Paolozzi Revealed

A Masterclass with

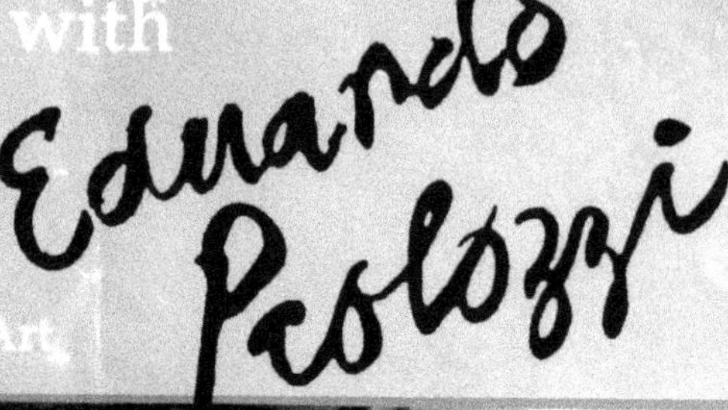

15 - 26 July 1996
Edinburgh College of Art

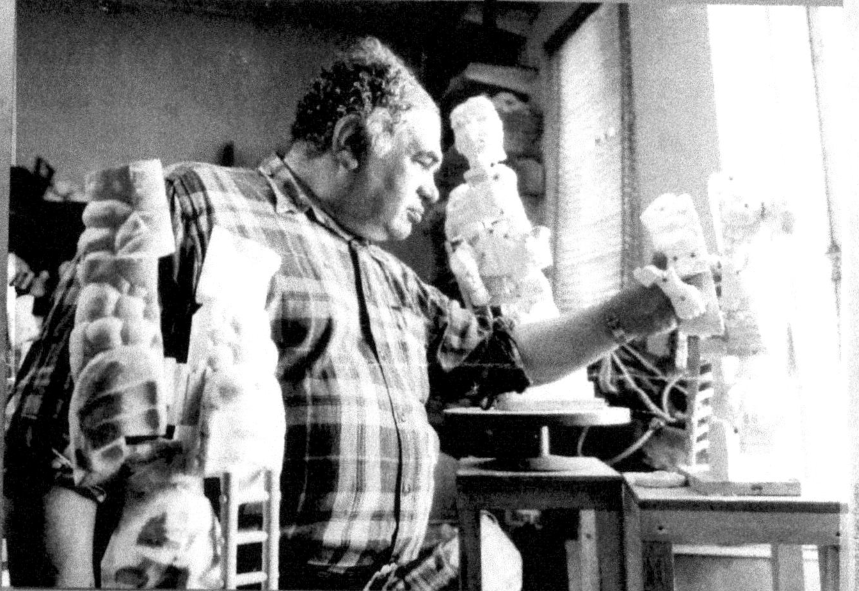

THE TRANSLATION OF EXPERIENCE

A Synthesis of Graphics and Sculpture

A two-week Masterclass with

Sir Eduardo Paolozzi

For course details and application forms contact: Director, Centre for Continuing Studies, Edinburgh College of Art, Lauriston Place, Edinburgh EH3 9DF
Telephone: 0131-221 6111 Fax: 0131-221 6109

Edinburgh College of Art
Heriot-Watt University

Paolozzi Revealed

Ten days with a creative Titan

Ann Shaw

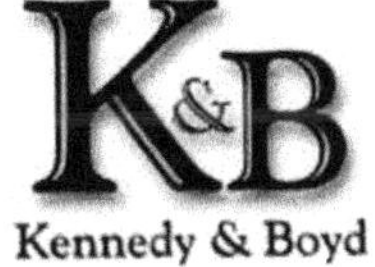

Kennedy & Boyd
an imprint of
Zeticula Ltd
Unit 13
196 Rose Street
Edinburgh
EH2 4AT
Scotland

http://www.kennedyandboyd.co.uk
admin@kennedyandboyd.co.uk

First published in 2015

ISBN 978-1-84921-149-9

I dedicate this book
to the memory of
Sir Eduardo Paolozzi,
KBE, RA (1924-2005)

Acknowledgements

I would like to thank
my former work colleague, Lesley Duncan, Poetry Editor of the Glasgow Herald, for her help, support and encouragement, my husband, Malcolm Shaw – for digitising the photographs – and George Sutherland for proof-reading the book.
Special thanks to Judith Collins for her brilliant biography, **Paolozzi**, *from which I quote in the introduction.*

I would also like to thank all the students who took part in this Masterclass.
The participants were (at the time of the class):
Gavin Adams
Postgraduate in printmaking at the Royal College of Art.
Jean Anderson
Graduate Edinburgh University in Sociology. Undertaken courses at Edinburgh Sculpture Workshop.
Vince Briffa
Based in Malta. Exhibited internationally, works as graphic designer running a company that specialises in TV computer graphics.
Marion Campbell
Mature student, in her final year of the Fine Art degree at Liverpool John Moores University. Works in clay.
Sheila Darlington
Lived in Africa, works as a designer for the National Youth Music Theatre, currently designing their Edinburgh Festival

production of The Beggars' Opera.
Antony Dufort
Read history at New College Oxford then art at Chelsea. Self-taught sculptor.
Sara Evans
Post graduate in Printmaking at the Royal College of Art.
Mo Farquharson
Trained at the Ruskin School, then at the Massachusetts College of Art. Works full time as a sculptor, undertaking commissions.
Lida Hatrick
Born in Czech Republic. Has MA in English and Russian at Edinburgh University and an MSc in linguistics. Has undertaken evening classes in sculpture at ECA for 5 years.
Camilla Le May
Undergraduate in Fine Art, University of Edinburgh. Taken evening classes at college in art for three years.
Graham Maule
Graduate of Glasgow School of Art in architecture.
Diana Nelson
Reading for an MA in Art and Design at Leeds.
Martin Nelson
Former consultant orthopaedic surgeon at Leeds General Hospital now taking a part-time degree in Fine Art at Sheffield University.
Anna Ricketts
Undergraduate student at Camberwell, now doing joint honours in Sculpture and Ceramics. Also self-employed as a gilder, restorer and specialist decorator.
Ann Shaw
Artist and journalist. Has taken a wide range of courses, including Edinburgh College of Art Summer School and several courses at Glasgow School of Art. Works as a journalist on The Glasgow Herald.
Jane Summers
Graduate from Sydney College of Arts in sculpture, performance and installation.
Allan Thompson
Retired from business life, has undertaken a wide range of art courses and hopes to take a full time art degree.
Diana Thompson
Trained at Kingston Poly as a mature student, has exhibited widely, including the Commonwealth Institute and the Royal Academy.

Contents

Preface

In 1995, when the art historian Judith Collins asked the sculptor Eduardo Paolozzi how he was, he replied: "Edging towards immortality." Was it tongue-in-cheek? She does not know.

A year later I signed up for his Masterclass at Edinburgh College of Art. This rare opportunity to work with one of the great artists of the 20th century came about by pure serendipity, something that Paolozzi himself would have approved of. After a career in journalism, latterly with *The Glasgow Herald*, I had decided in mid-life to fulfil the dream of becoming an artist. For years I had attended numerous day and evening classes, workshops and summer schools, in Scotland and London, and I had even taken a month's Sabbatical at a painting school in France.

So when I heard that Paolozzi was going to run a class at Edinburgh College of Art I put my name forward. Potential candidates were asked to submit a statement of why they wanted to study with him and if he liked what was said they would be accepted.

Thus on Saturday July 15 1996 I began ten days of working with Paolozzi. These days would have a greater influence on me than any time I was later to spend as a student at Glasgow School of Art and the School of the Art Institute in Chicago. Paolozzi asked us to keep a diary of our time with him. What follows is an unabridged account of his Masterclass.

How will history view him? He died in 2005, and the publication in 2014 of the monograph

Paolozzi*, by Judith Collins, places him firmly among the great European artists of the 20th century, alongside Giacometti, Leger, Jean Arp, Tristan Tzara, Brancusi, Dubuffet and Braque, all of whom he had met while working in Paris in the 1940s.

He was born in Leith, Edinburgh, in 1924, to Italian parents who ran a shop. There was little to indicate in his early years that he would one day become one of the outstanding sculptors of the 20th century. His influence can still be seen today among younger generations of graphic artists as they seek to illustrate the world of technology, which so fascinated Paolozzi, a world where man and machine are beginning to mesh and robots play an increasingly important role in our lives.

Some of his key sculptures illustrate this well. They include "The Artist as Hephaestus" (now in a private collection) – a self portrait where he sees himself in the guise of the Greek god of technology, fire and metal, "Vulcan" – a huge welded steel plate sculpture which occupies the central area of the Dean Gallery (in the Scottish National Gallery of Modern Art), and "Newton after Blake" outside the British Library, London.

Many people will be familiar with the Tottenham Court Road Underground mosaics in London (1986) and his colourful collages. He was known as the King of British Pop Art, a label he strenuously denied, not surprisingly since his work encompassed a far greater breadth of vision than pop culture. An incorrigible collector, he revealed in his studios a magpie-like mind, stretching from tribal art to the detritus of modern packaging, which he later incorporated into his vast collection of collages and prints.

On one hand he seemed to be an outsider, a maverick, a European not fitting easily into the British art establishment, until in his later years they finally embraced this working-class Italian-Scot and showered accolades on him. He became Her Majesty's Sculptor in Ordinary for Scotland in 1986 and was knighted KBE in 1988.

Paolozzi was a European long before it became fashionable or acceptable. He knew from an early age that he had to reach beyond Scotland, then England, if he was to fulfil his potential. And so for a number of years he worked in Paris, America and Germany.

Yet it is clear from his enormous body of work that this complex artist and unique cultural figure was indeed working at the heart of the British establishment, a man who knew how to network long before the term became widely used, a sculptor making accessible art for the public domain, linking the past with the present and foretelling in some prescient way our futures driven by technology.

**Paolozzi,* Judith Collins, 2014, Ashgate (Lund Humphries), ISBN 978-1-84822-131-4. Published with support from the Paul Mellon Centre for Studies in British Art.

Day One

"You will learn by a process of osmosis"

- *Paolozzi*

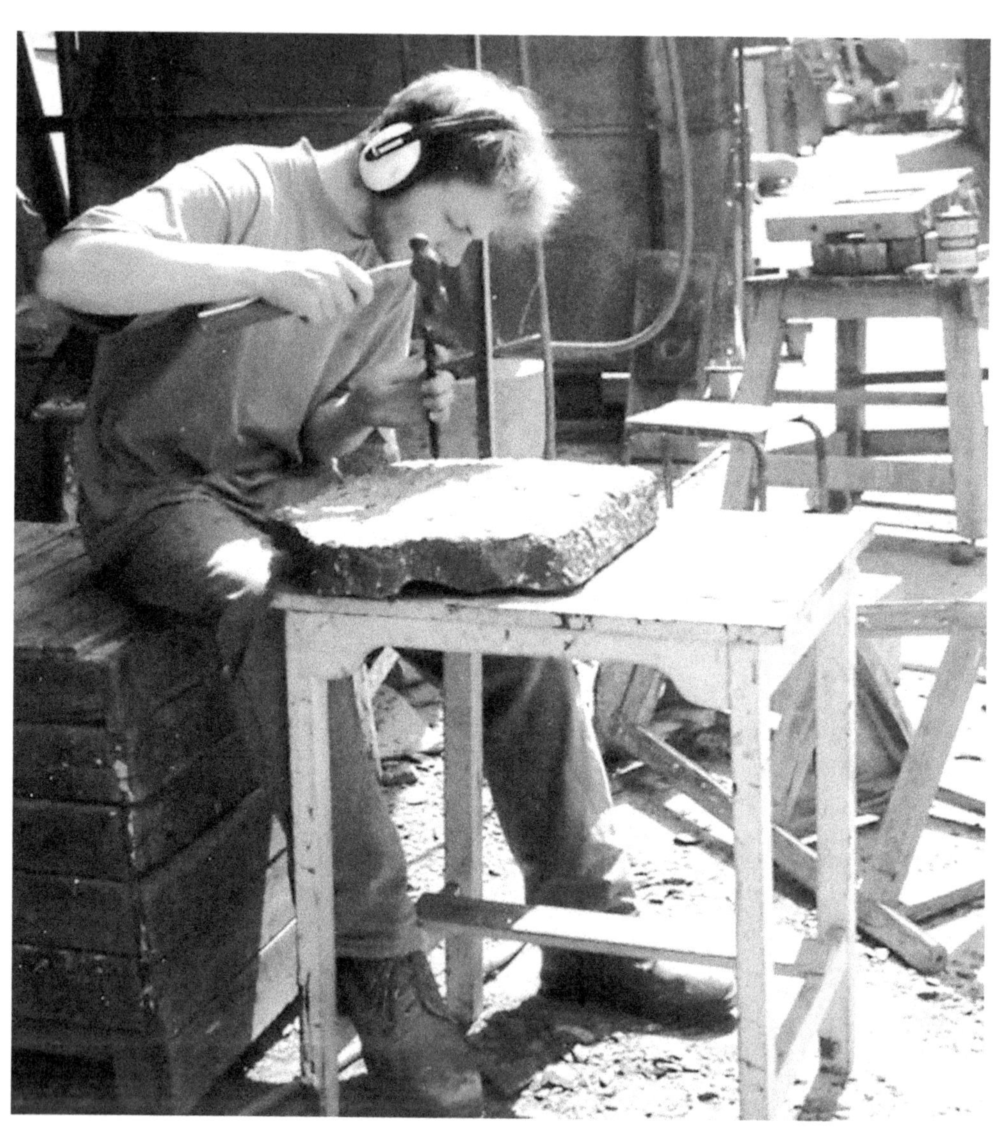

Gradually we find our own space ...

We await the arrival of Eduardo Paolozzi, the grand old man of British sculpture, with whom we are going to work over the next ten days. Standing in the big, white, empty sculpture studio of Edinburgh College of Art I glance around at my fellow students. We're a mixed bunch. Some are professional artists and art students while the rest fall into two categories: a retired teacher, doctor, and surgeon and 'others'. I fall into the 'others' category – a journalist about to give up work with *The Glasgow Herald* to go as a mature student to Glasgow School of Art. Am I making a mistake? Will I regret it?

But where is Paolozzi? It's 9.30 am and Geraldine Prince, art historian and course organiser arrives. "His flight from Paris has been delayed. I suggest you all go and have a coffee."

En route to the café I see a poster advertising **A Masterclass with Paolozzi**, and a student has scribbled on it: **"***Be afraid...be very afraid***."** We sit and drink coffee. "Do you think he is as ferocious as his reputation says?", I ask a bearded young man next to me. He nods. Geraldine hands us a programme for the next ten days with the caveat: "He may well tear all this up once he sees it". (He does.)

We are just digesting this when a tired, heavily-built old man wanders in. It's Paolozzi. "I have been up since 5 o'clock this morning," he growls, sitting in the empty seat next to me. Geraldine rushes to get him a cup of coffee. He takes it without a word of thanks.

"I was wondering what you had in mind for our students." Geraldine is the epitome of Edinburgh politeness. Paolozzi snarls, without bothering to look at her: "I am not going to be pushed around by you or anybody."

An uneasy silence falls over the café. "Get back to the studio. I will see you in five minutes." We shuffle to our feet and walk back. Nobody speaks.

A few minutes later he joins us and without any social niceties launches straight into a history of 20th century art, until he sees Geraldine lurking in a corner. "Surrealism was a major force…" He stops. "You can get back to your office and do some more faxes, or whatever it is that you do." Geraldine leaves, trying to make a joke of her dismissal: "I know when I'm not wanted."

There are no chairs. We stand for one hour while Paolozzi continues with a lecture on modern art. He reminds us of the importance of plaster casts and the wonderful drawings made by people such as Seurat and laments the fact that colleges are throwing them out. "They still have a part to play in our visual vocabulary," he says.

He gallops through his career spanning over 50 years picking out highlights. He says he hated art school, particularly the Slade, and couldn't wait to leave – though he did like his time in Edinburgh. He went to Paris in the late 1940s in order to be among real artists. He says: "It is important to be in the presence of other artists where a process akin to osmosis takes place. I am a great believer in that, after all that's how all the great art of the Renaissance was produced, not in art colleges but in big studios."

He lists artists he met in Paris, Giacometti, Leger, and it reads like a *Who's Who of Modern Art.* You realise you are in the presence of a key figure in the world of sculpture, a living link with a turning point in modern art. He speaks about the importance of paper, and the handmade paper from Japan through to the Renaissance, "because of the quality of the natural materials the drawings of Goya and Rembrandt have stood the test of time."

He talks about his own work and current projects, which include a double-life-sized figure for Kew Gardens and the refurbishing of Edinburgh's Dean Centre which will be dedicated to his work and include a garden for the blind. He said there would be a shop selling proper wooden toys, not pencils from Taiwan.

Now the lecture takes a philosophical turn. He tells us of his interest in the relationship between literature and sculpture and how countless works of art are in fact inspired by great masterpieces. He quotes Ovid's *Metamorphoses*. He says that a glance around the National Gallery shows how pagan themes and religious subjects have fired the imagination of artists throughout the ages. Lots of artists need literature to stimulate the creative process.

He adds that Surrealism played an important role in helping to amalgamate so many diverse things and he believes we are in for a big revival of surrealism. He recommends we look at the work of Kurt Schwitters (1887-1948), a German artist famous for his collages, who showed that it is possible to make art out of everyday objects, provided one is an artist. One of the wonderful things about Surrealism is that it is all-embracing; anything goes. All kinds of art outside orthodox opinion are accepted, from primitive to psychotic art and bad movies, even anonymous erotic art.

Finally he concludes by announcing that he will be doing his own work alongside us in the studio and hints: "You will learn by a process of osmosis." What on earth does that mean?

He looks around the group and booms: "Now you start." Then in a piece of pure theatre he turns his back on the class. We are left staring at the posterior of the bulky, crumpled form of Paolozzi.

We look at each other, shocked into silence. The studio is empty, the walls are blank. There are no materials, no information. Nothing. The panic going through the class is palpable. We had expected to be told what to do, to be given projects.

I am glad that I had taken the precaution, fearing something like this might happen, of stuffing the boot of my car with a collection of 'found objects'.

Earlier we had learnt that Paolozzi had approached Edinburgh College of Art asking if he could do a Masterclass. Two previous ones had

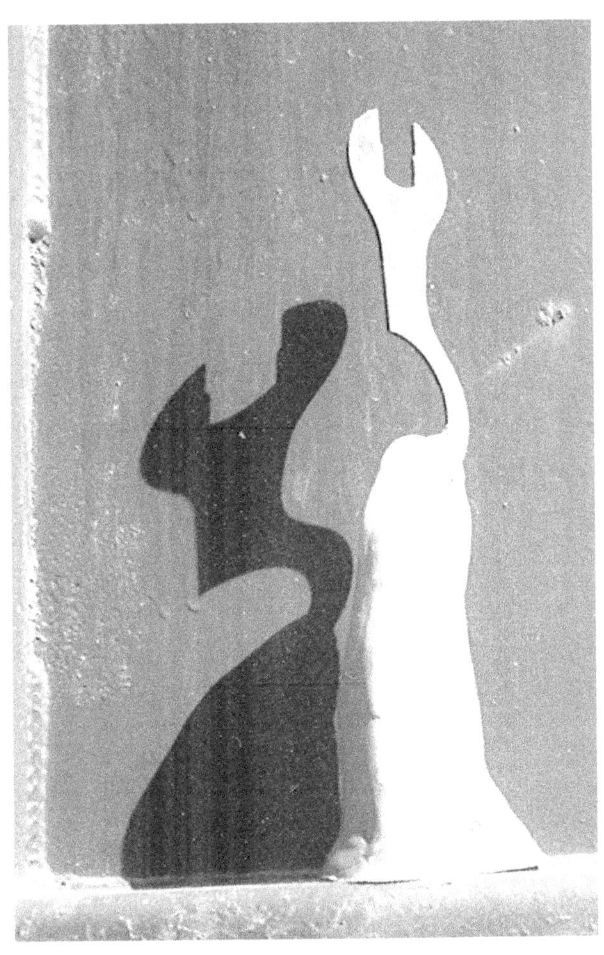

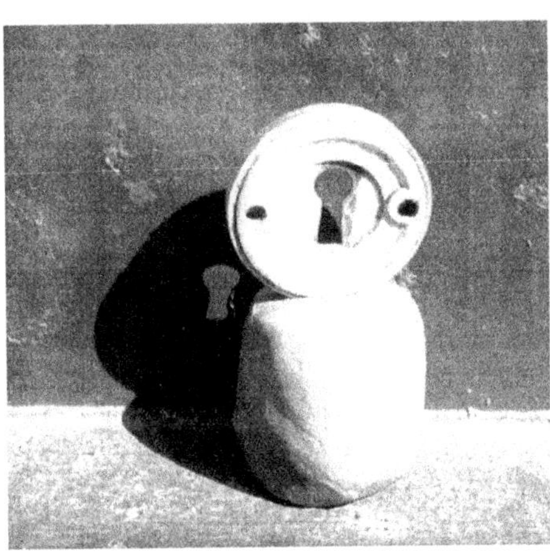

... I had taken the precaution, fearing something like this might happen, of stuffing the boot of my car with a collection of 'found objects'.

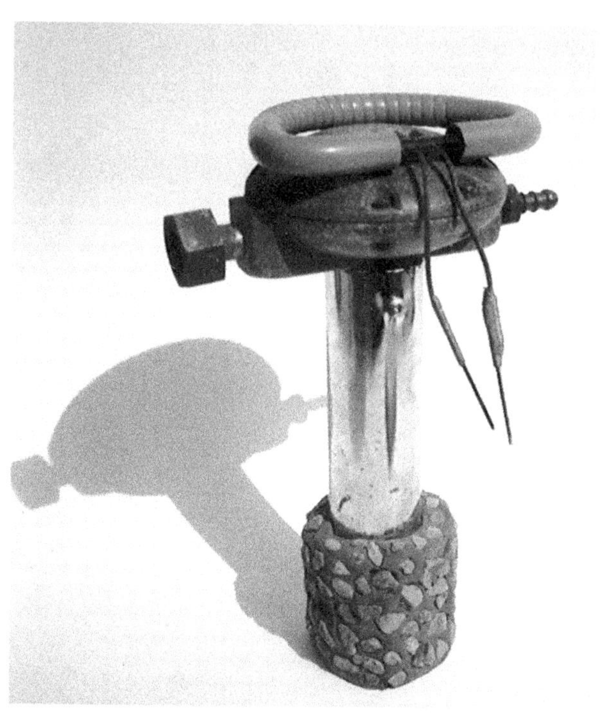

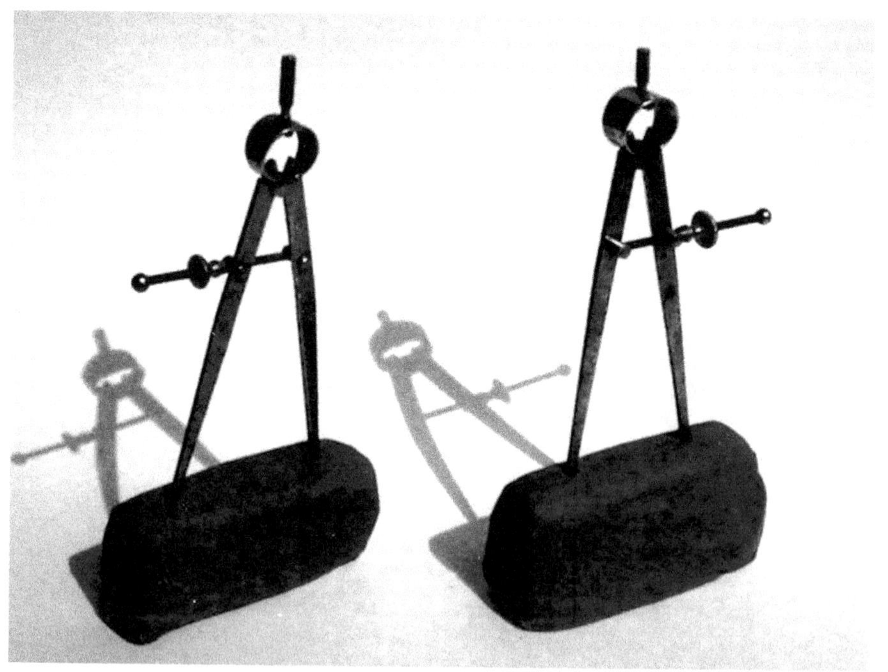

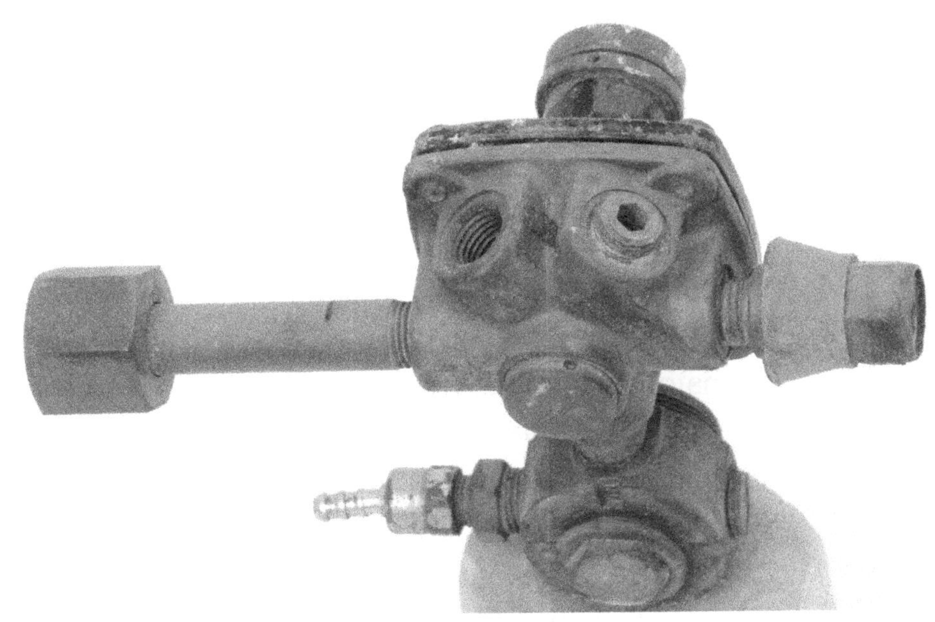

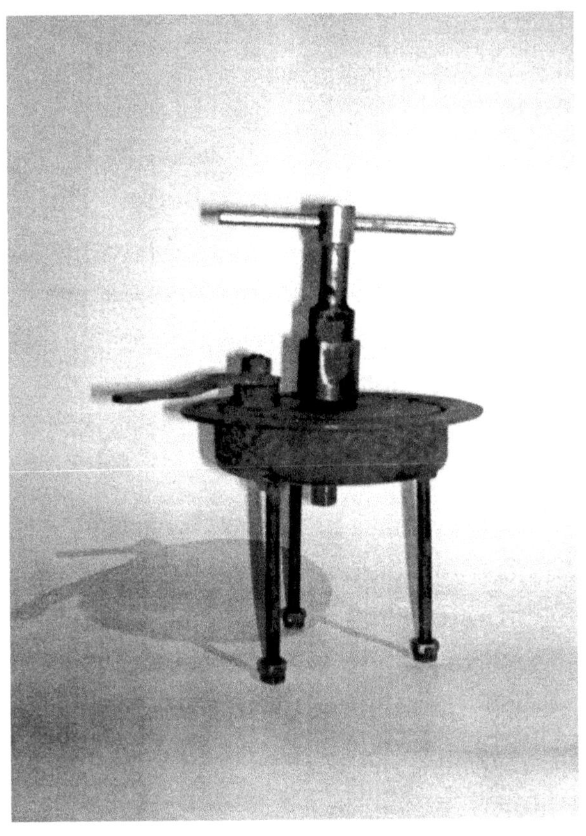

Some 'ready-mades' or assemblages constructed from tools in the back of my car.
These objects reveal my fascination with robots and the role they already played in transforming our society.

been unsuccessful. (With hindsight, that should have been a warning to us.) One in Hamburg turned out to be for the 'ladies who lunch', those who would buy a Picasso drawing and would like to be able to say that they have been to a Paolozzi Masterclass. The second in Ireland had organisational problems.

Gradually we find our own space, a table, some materials from the back of the sculpture workshop – or, in my case, a box of old tools from the boot of the car – and I spend the rest of the day making assemblages out of found objects, modern 'fetishes'.

He joins our table for lunch. Once we have overcome our fear of him we begin to ask him questions.

"What do you think of Damien Hirst?" I ask. Instead of a direct answer he says: "He has a strong dealer." (Jay Joplin of the White Cube.) "But is it art?"

"Art covers a very broad field today. Museums and galleries are getting closer," says Paolozzi. He adds: "Do you know that the Natural History Museum has a spirit room that includes a baby rhinoceros?"

"How does that differ from the work of Hirst?" I persist. "It doesn't," he replies. But he refuses to be drawn on the work of Hirst.

The name of a certain shop in Soho, that specializes in leather underwear for transvestites, comes up in the conversation. I giggle. Paolozzi spots this: "You know the shop?"

"Er, no..." I sense his disdain of my provincialism.

After lunch we were just settling down to work when his voice boomed out:

"I am going to do a monoprint demonstration." It was a spontaneous happening. Even those among us who were experienced printmakers, and there were a few, felt obliged to down tools to watch the maestro at work.

The demo over, I was en route back to my place when Paolozzi's voice rang out in my direction: "Draw!" I had nothing in my hand. I looked round, panic-stricken, for a pen or a brush or any kind of implement.

"No, with your hand." Now, drawing is my biggest weakness, and suddenly to have to do it under the eye of Paolozzi, watched by a group of artists who were clearly in a league far beyond me. This is the kind of experience that nightmares are made of.

What to do? Seeing some black printer's ink nearby I thrust my hand into it and make some expressionistic marks on the pristine white A1 paper Paolozzi is holding. He nods, a sign I take to be of approval.

Slowly we realise we are learning from him but not in the way we had expected.

Mid-afternoon, a fair-haired good-looking young man walked into the studio with a very heavy suitcase.

"What's that?" I whisper as he passes my table.

"It's Paolozzi's work."

He is Paolozzi's assistant, a recent graduate from the Royal College of Art. He puts it on a table underneath the window in the next door studio and opens it up. It's full of sketches, drawings and *maquettes*. No wonder he needed someone young and strong to carry it. And that's where Paolozzi sits all week, talking, thinking, and sketching.

He gives out postcards, and catalogues of his work. "You can keep them," he says. We make an undignified scramble for the contents of the suitcase.

Towards the end of the afternoon I become aware of a dark presence, of somebody hovering over my right shoulder. It's Paolozzi. He's looking at my work. "You photograph them ... tomorrow." And he walks away. It was a flashbulb moment. Until then I had not thought of photography as an art form, I used it simply to document my work.

Paolozzi is very much the maestro and we follow him from studio to cafe like devout disciples. Walking back, following our afternoon tea break in the college cafe, we pass the college library. Paolozzi throws out a challenge: "Why don't you go in there and read some books on me then ask some questions?" He doesn't wait for an answer. He marches straight back to the studio. In the days that follow we do begin to question him. Oh yes, he told us to keep a diary and he would read it at the end, "I will give a special prize for the best student's work."

Day Two

“All human experience is just one big collage.”

- Paolozzi

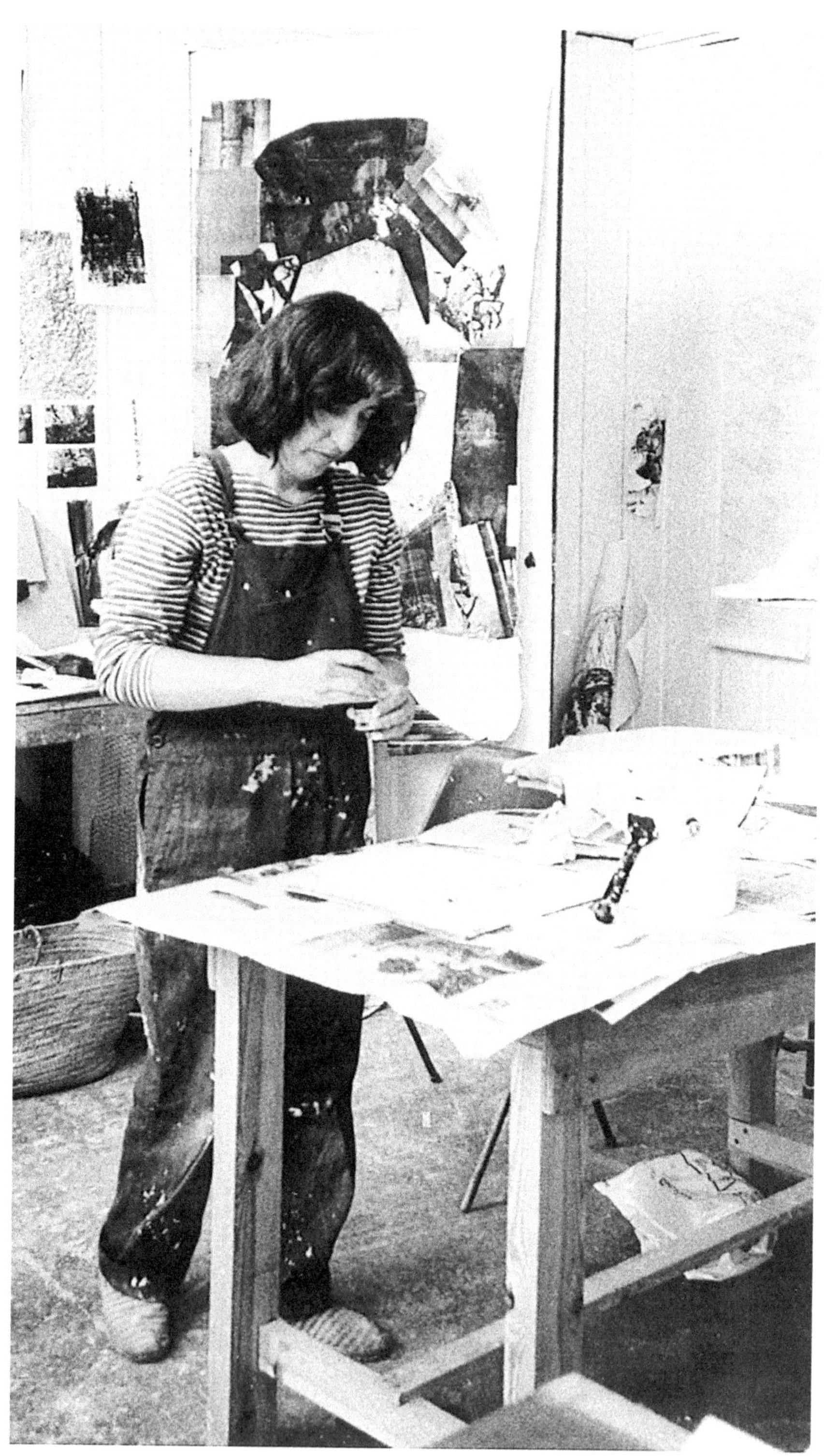

One or two are heard to murmur that they would have liked more direction; they would have liked to be told what to do.

I am busy arranging my ‘assemblages’- old industrial tools which I have gathered over the past few months in anticipation of working with Paolozzi, on a wall near the entrance to Edinburgh College of Art when a black cab draws up and Paolozzi tumbles out.

Rumour has it he has a personal fitness trainer but we dare not ask. He’s overweight. He sees me.

“Shadows ... remember the shadows,” he says without stopping merely throwing a glance in my direction. He adds: “Take slides.”

Paolozzi doesn’t waste time on social chitchat; not for him the small talk that oils the wheels of social interaction. Later we all meet up in the canteen for our coffee break, and already there is a certain edginess, developing amongst the group, to see who gets to sit close to him. We fear him yet he fascinates us. He has an aura that sets him apart, a charisma that both hypnotises and frightens us.

He is standing at the food counter and suddenly he picks up the biscuit basket and proffers it around the gathered students. “Have one on me.” Our fingers plunge into the basket. And I think, for the first time, maybe he does have a soft side after all.

Encouraged by this, I ask him about the use of metamorphism in his work. “Yes, I do ... do you have a problem with that?” he snaps.

“Of course not!” I bluster, though I am surprised at his harsh reply. Worse follows: “Have you read Franz Kafka’s *The Metamorphosis*?”

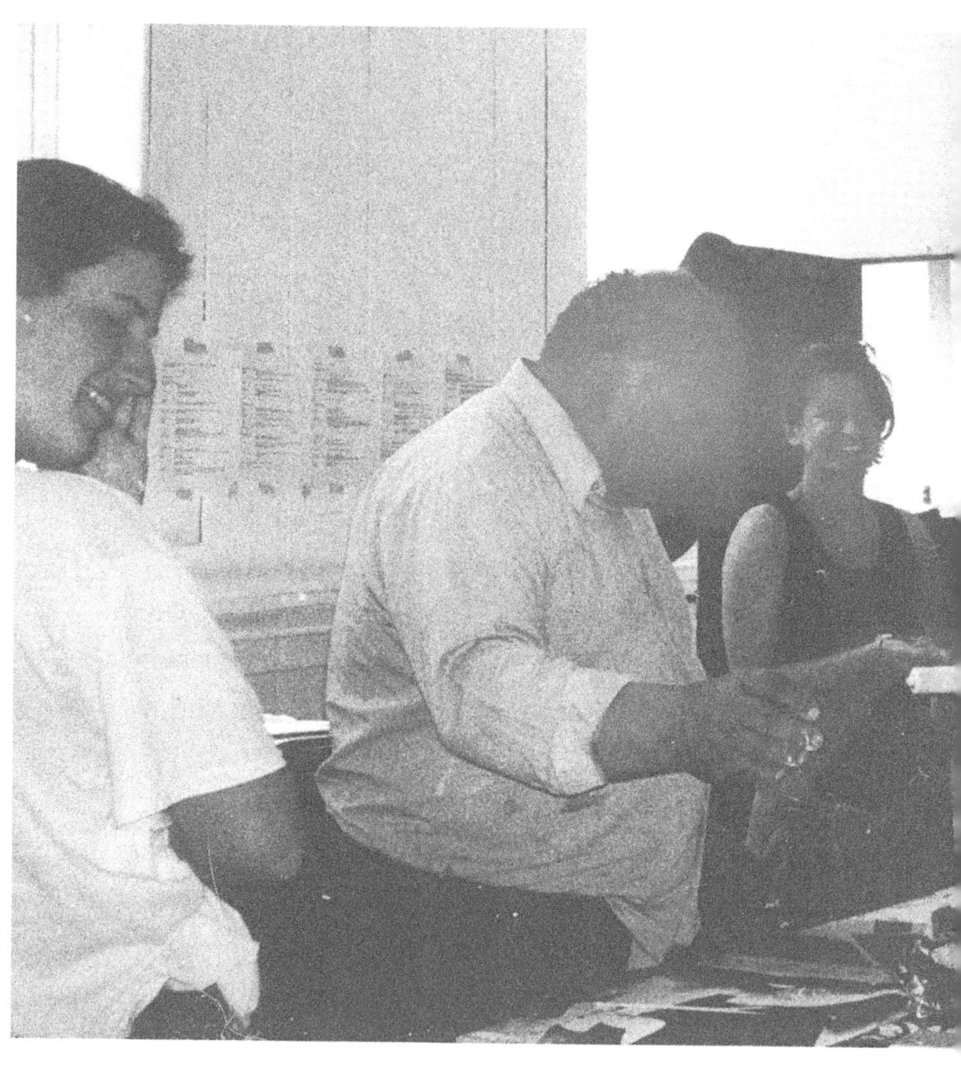

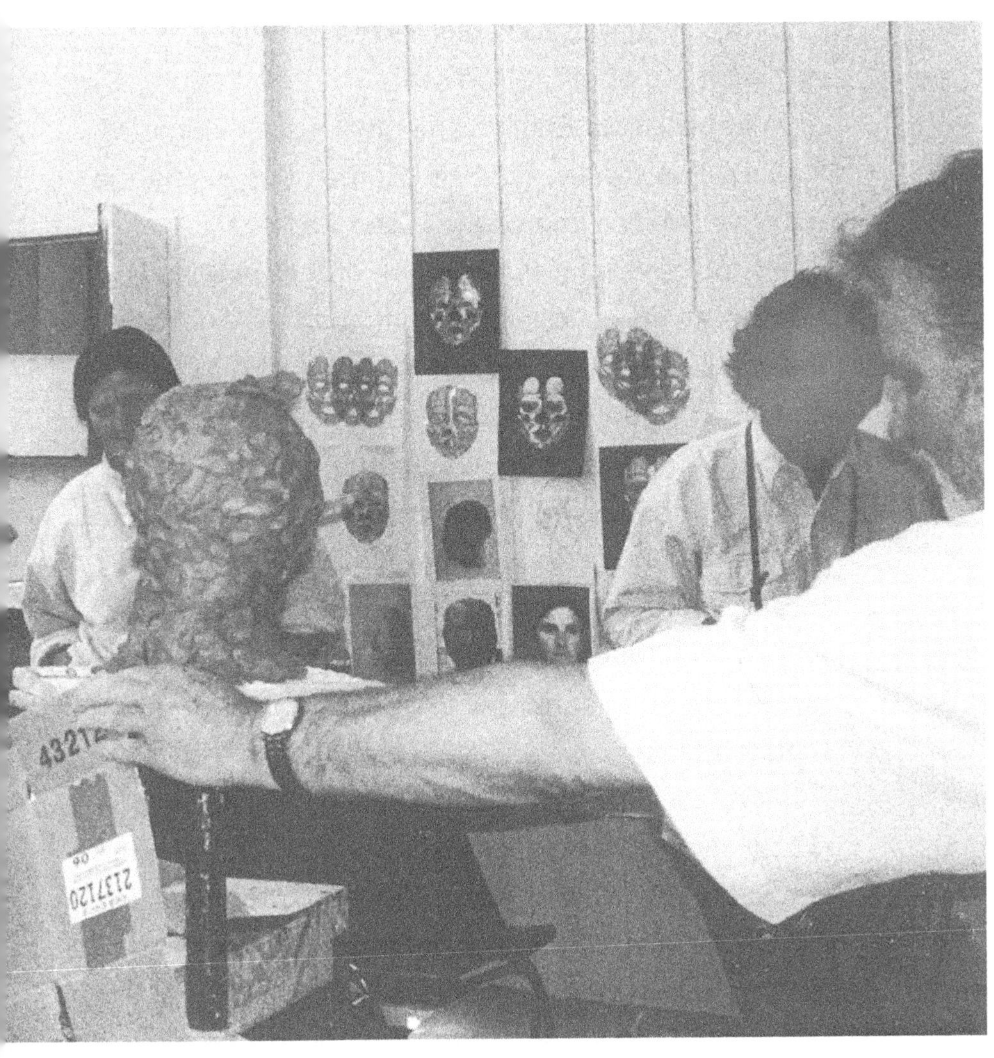

Paolozzi examines some students' work

"Er.... no." Of course I have heard of it, even tried to read it, but I am ashamed to admit I hadn't. Paolozzi turns to the rest of the group around the table. "Have any of you read it?"

Lida, a young Czech woman says "I have."

"Tell them about it," he said.

In impeccable English she gives us a resumé of Kafka's *The Metamorphosis.* Some of us exchange glances. We are impressed. Even Paolozzi.

He looks around the canteen at the bare walls: "This is an art college and what have they got on the walls? Nothing!" He spots a vase of plastic flowers on the windowsill. "Disgusting!" Another student points out that at least the ones on the food counter are real. Paolozzi snorts.

After lunch we are all marched off to the library to look at the internet, still a new phenomenon (this is 1996 after all). There is a technical problem; nobody is quite sure how to access it except one man in the library. It's all very creaky.

I am fascinated by the technology. Paolozzi is dismissive. "It is only a tool."

"But a very powerful tool," I say, disappointed in Paolozzi's reaction. For an artist with a reputation resting to a great extent on the way he had recognized the impact of technology in our lives I had looked for a more enthusiastic response.

The other students side with Paolozzi. "What's this got to do with art? It's not proper art." A discussion of sorts takes place, then I realise I have no support for my views, so I ask the technician if I could call up the web site of the Society of Scottish Artists, which I had been responsible for initiating, making it the first artist web site to go online in the UK.

"Here, take a seat," he says, glad to hand over to someone else. The computer is slow, and it takes a while to load. Eventually on screen appears the 1995 Society of Scottish Artists' annual exhibition.

Surely they would be impressed with the potential of the technology now? Not a bit. So our visit to witness cutting-edge technology in the college library is met with silence and we make our way back to the studios.

One or two are heard to murmur that they would have liked more direction; they would have liked to be told what to do. George Donald, artist, lecturer and co-director of the course, tries to explain that is not what a Masterclass is all about. "Anyway, it's not the way Paolozzi operates."

That evening we are shown a film about the development of pop art, and we are puzzled why Paolozzi does not feature in it. It traced the development through the mass media, advertising, movies, and graphics in attempts to reject the establishment of Fine Art personified by Herbert Read. One characteristic of the Independent Group, of which Paolozzi was a founder member in 1952, was the strong link between popular culture and technology. But in 1955 the Independent Group faded away. There follows an exhibition at the Whitechapel, “This is Tomorrow”, dominated by a robot. To our surprise Paolozzi does not feature in this either.

Later he is asked in the discussion, “Why not?” The answer is simple: he refused to take part. One woman inquires if he would now like to tell us his side of the story. Paolozzi is uncomfortable with the question. “It’s too long ago… I have forgotten.”

But the woman persists. Paolozzi retaliates with a barbed swiftness. He turns to her and shouts. “Tell me, what do you remember from 40 years ago?”

Nothing more is said. There is an awkward silence. He had been asked an impossible question and he was not in the business of giving a few trite, facile comments. That is not his style. The course administrators, Geraldine Prince and George Donald, step into the uncomfortable silence and smooth over the situation.

That evening as I leave the college building I pick up one of the parking cones. Charlie, the janitor spots me. “Hey! That’s our property! You can’t have it.”

“Paolozzi says we must use found objects,” I say with new-found confidence. This is not quite true but I know he would never dare tackle the Grand Old Master of British sculpture.

In the days that follow I cover it with foil paper, decorate it with sweets and label it “Sweet Cone Named Desire”. It raises a few smiles in the studio though I sense they do not approve of my humour.

Art is meant to be serious.

Day Three

“ The golden rule is just to follow one’s obsessions.”

- *Paolozzi*

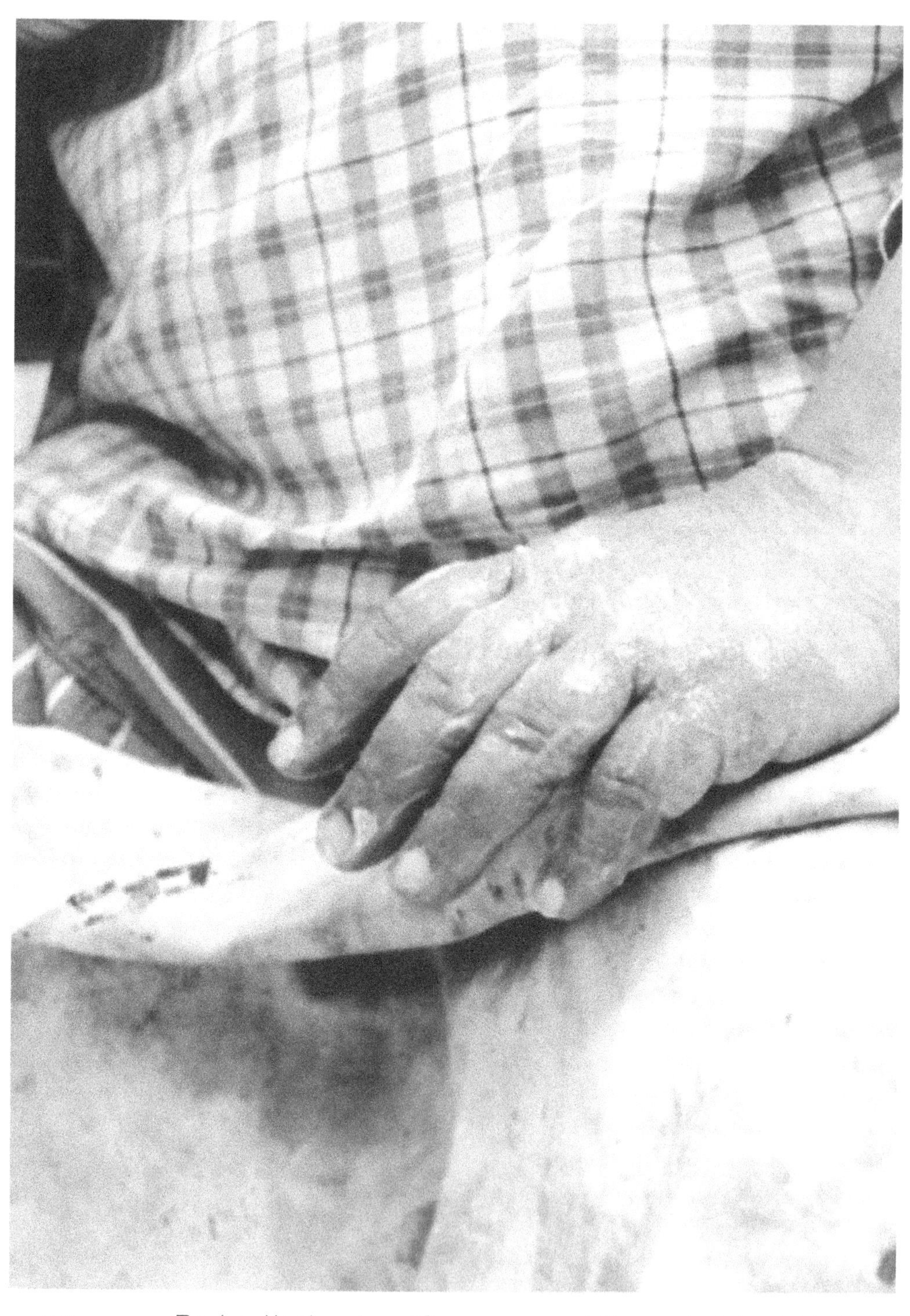

22 *Paolozzi looks at us. "Once you would have sketched this," he says. Suddenly there's a rush back to the studios to grab sketchbooks.*

I am alone with Paolozzi in the college café. The others have returned to the studios after lunch.

"Will you do something for me?" he says.

I'm surprised at the request but, ever the eager student wishing to ingratiate myself with the teacher, I nod.

He puts his hand into his pocket and pulls out a dirty, crumpled polythene bag full of small coins which he empties on to the table amidst the debris of dirty cups, plates and half eaten sandwiches. Amongst the coins is a carefully folded one-inch square piece of paper. He picks it up with his short, stubby fingers and delicately unfolds it. It is a German note.

"Will you take this to the bank and get it changed for me?"

" Yes, of course. How much is it?" He shrugs: "Maybe one or two hundred pounds, I don't know."

The bank gives me £400.

After some initial hiccups we have settled into a studio routine with each of us pursuing his or her own work though it is clear that some students had expected a more pro-active approach with Paolozzi maybe touring the studios and commenting on each person's work. He says he is unable to make a comment on our work until he sees what we do.

In the afternoon he announces he is going to the plaster workshop to have his hand cast in plaster and we are invited to watch. We drop what we are doing and scramble for good viewpoints with our cameras.

Paolozzi looks at us. "Once you would have sketched this," he says. Suddenly there's a rush back to the studios to grab sketchbooks.

Afterwards we are returning to the studio when Paolozzi stops in front of a large canvas at least 15 ft. x 15 ft. feet in the corridor, an abstract from the recent degree show waiting for its owner to collect. "What do you think of it?" he says. We are nonplussed. For the past couple of days we have passed it at least several times a day en route to the college café. We have grown used to it. We struggle to find something to say.

"It's very colourful!" ..."Vigorous brush strokes"... "Bold." "You can see De Kooning influence," says Mark, a graduate from the Royal College of Art and steeped in art history.

Paolozzi snaps: "You take it for granted. Once that would have been considered very controversial." We walk back to our studios in silence.

Our fears that he would turn out to be an arrogant egocentric, throwing his weight around in the studio, are disappearing. Still, we are in awe of him and dare not approach him without a good reason. Yet in the studio situation he is kind and gentle, reserving his vitriol for some unknown reason for Geraldine, art historian and course administrator, perhaps because she represents officialdom and bureaucracy, things he abhors, yet

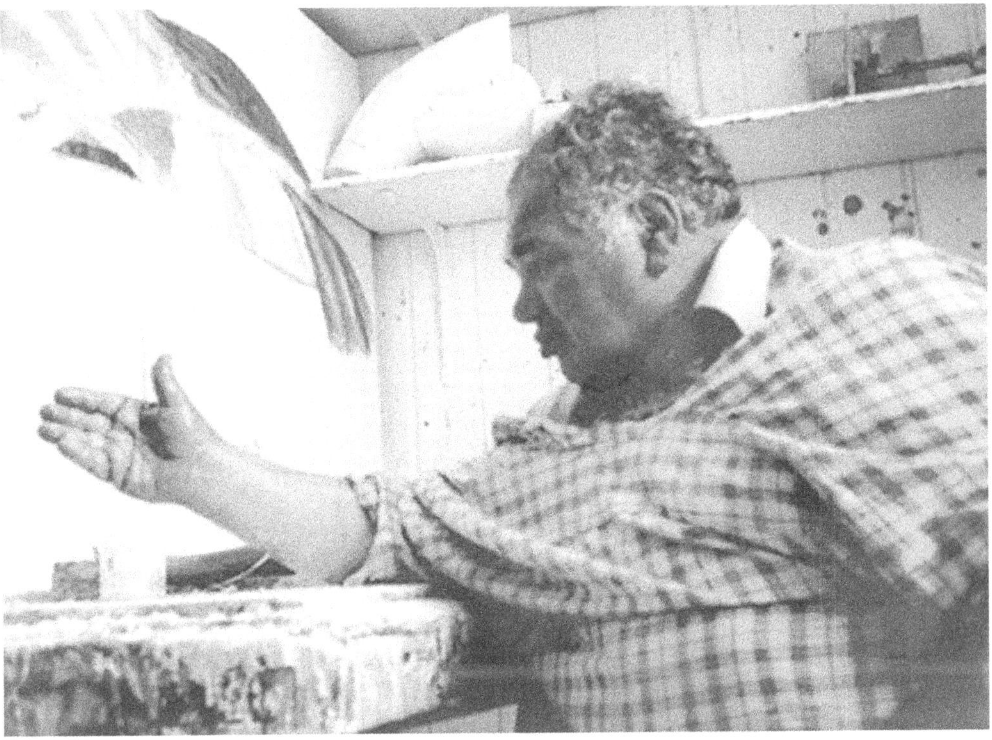

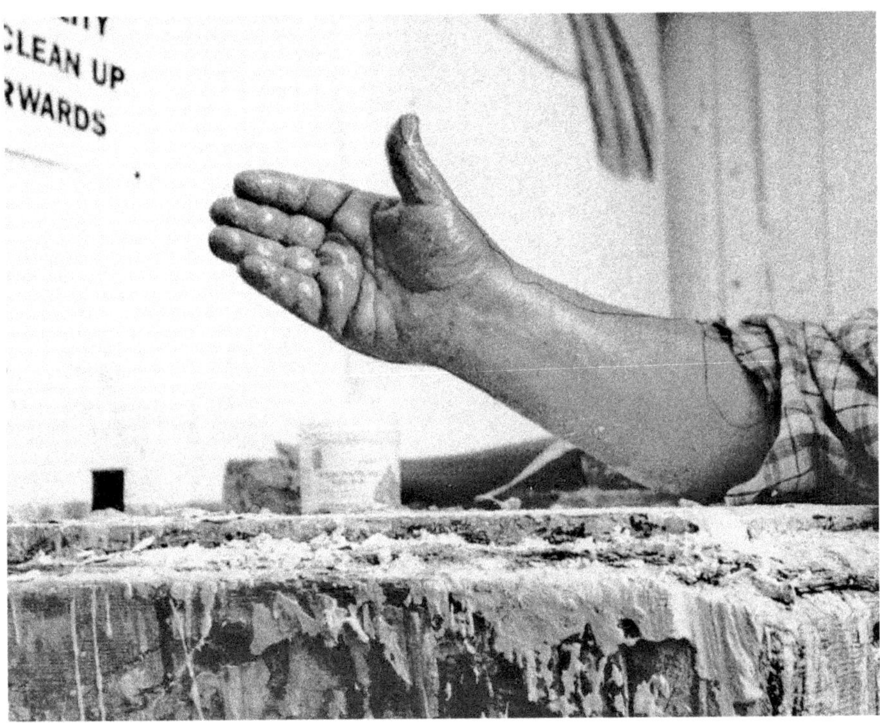

Paolozzi's hand is cast in plaster by a technician while students photograph and draw the process.

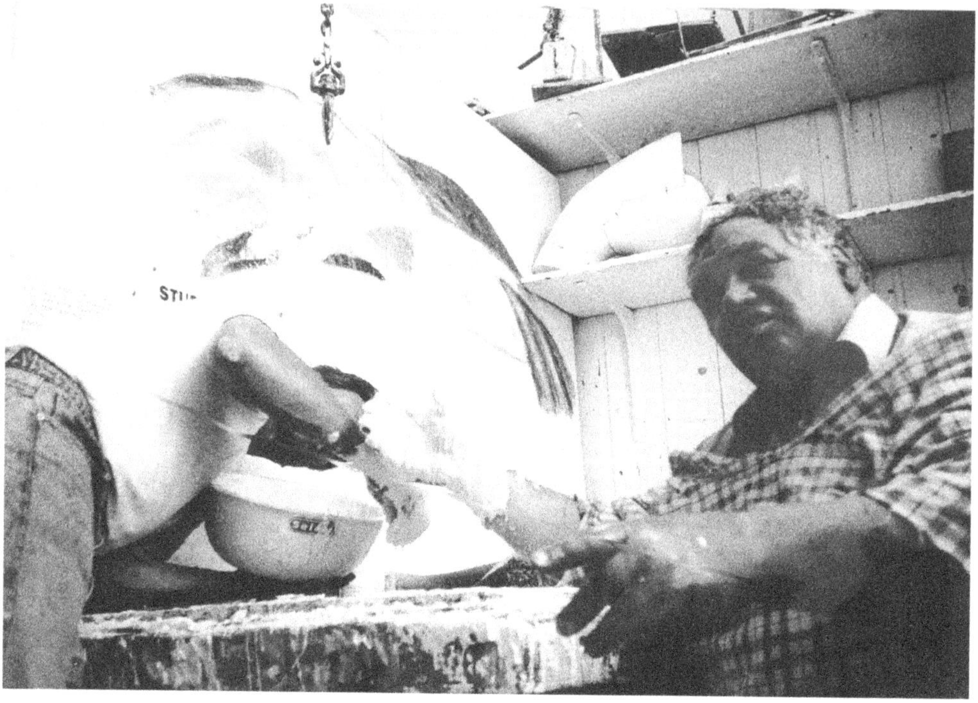

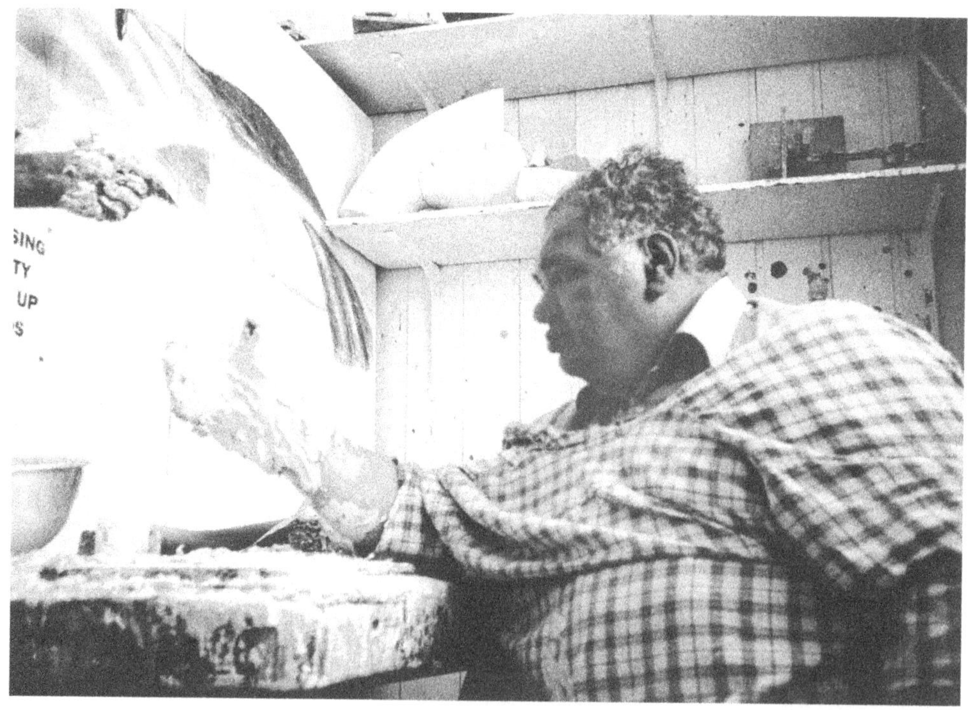

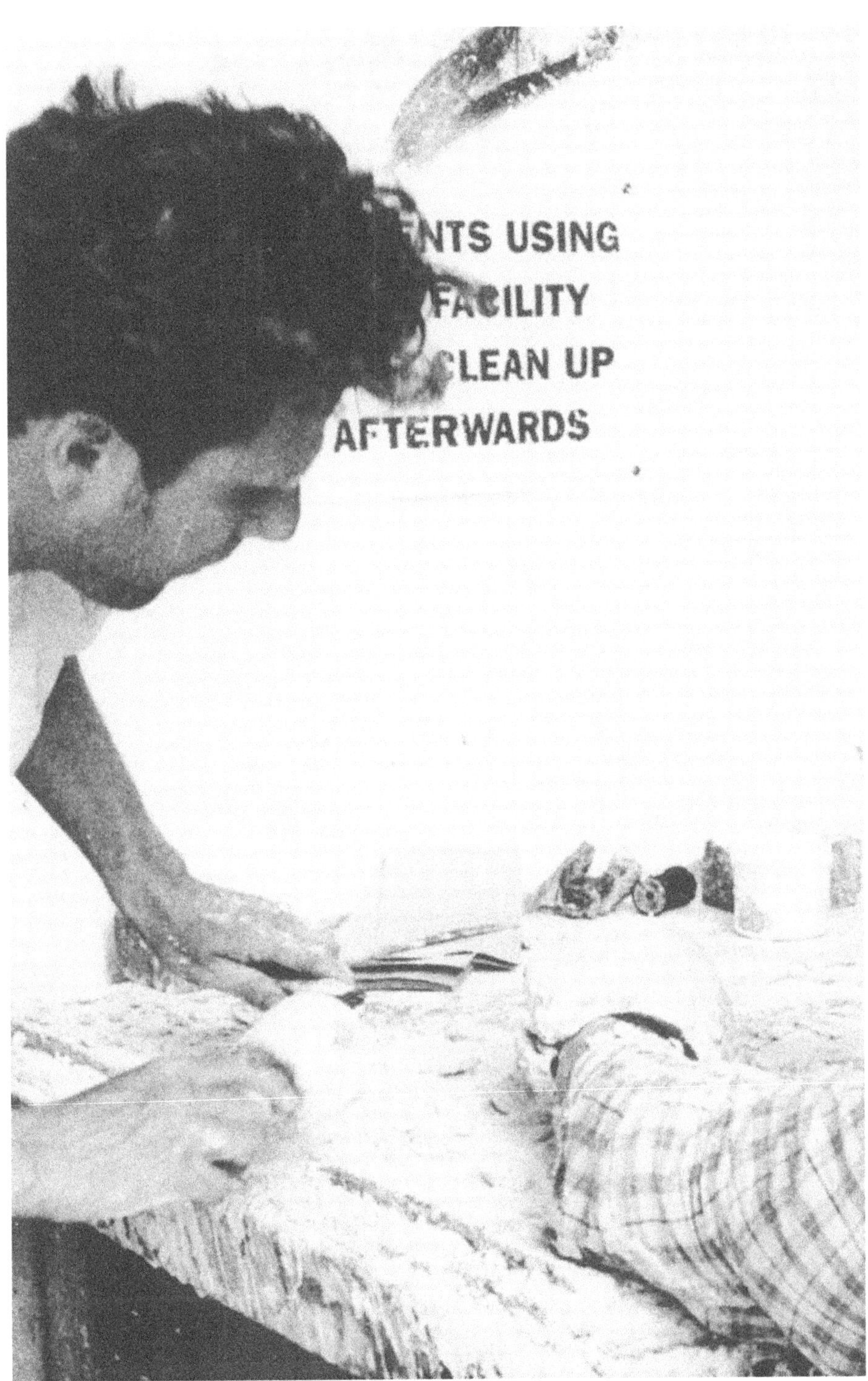
NTS USING
FACILITY
CLEAN UP
AFTERWARDS

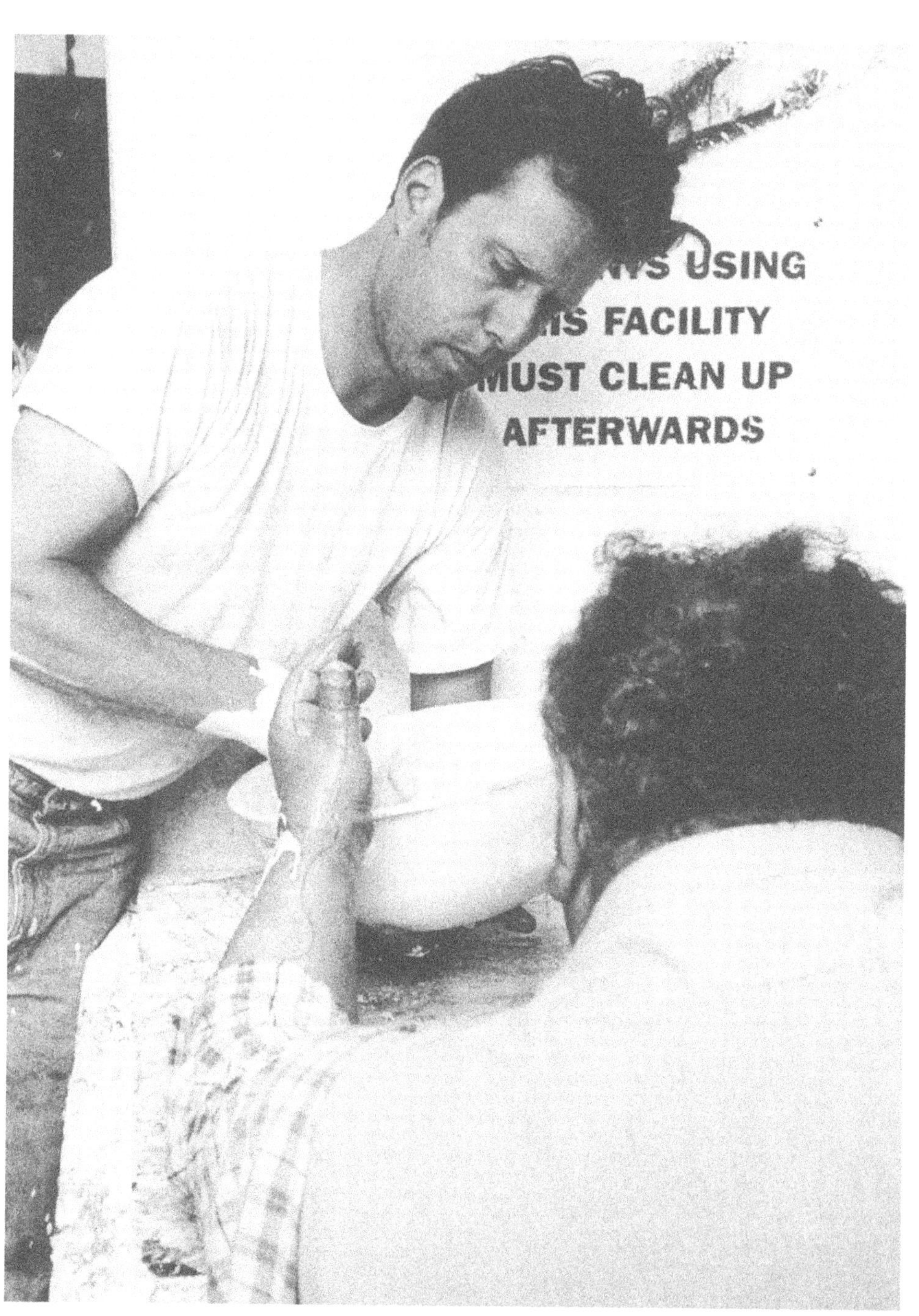
USING
FACILITY
MUST CLEAN UP
AFTERWARDS

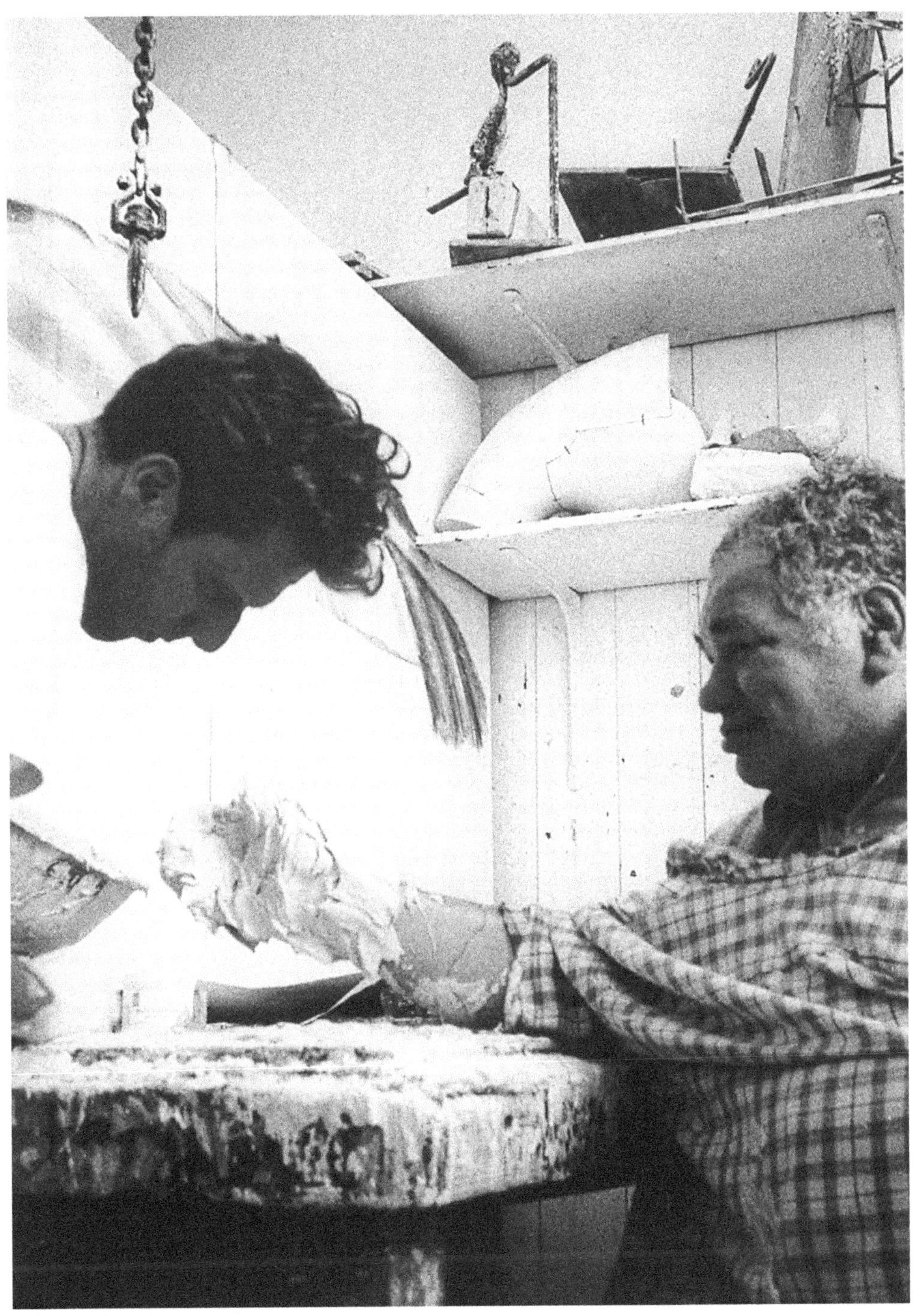

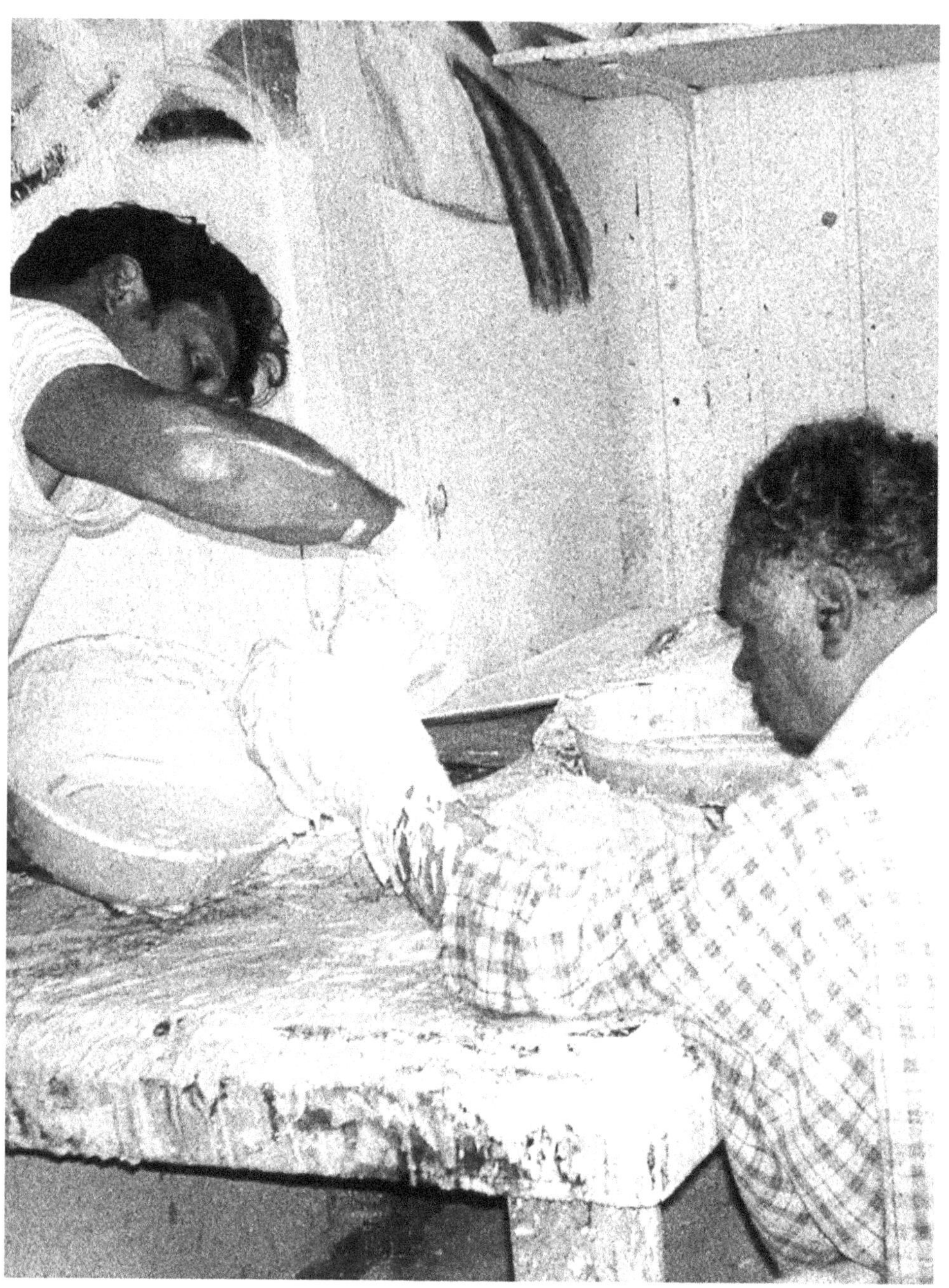

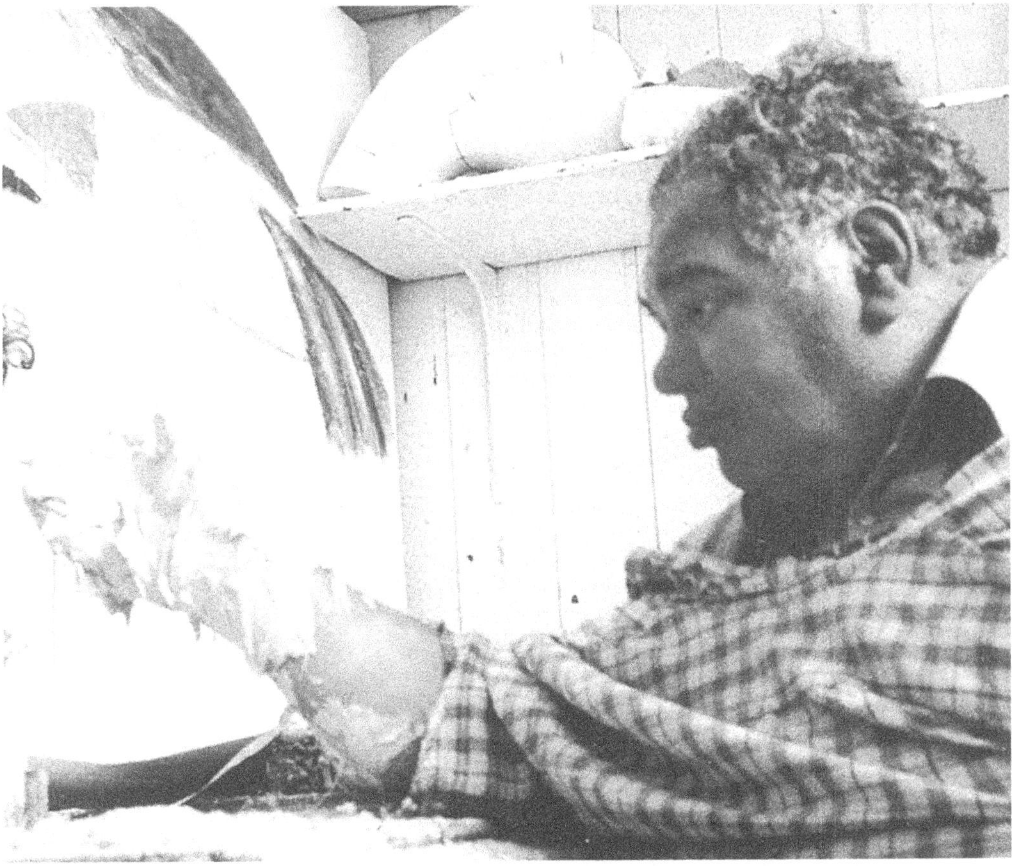

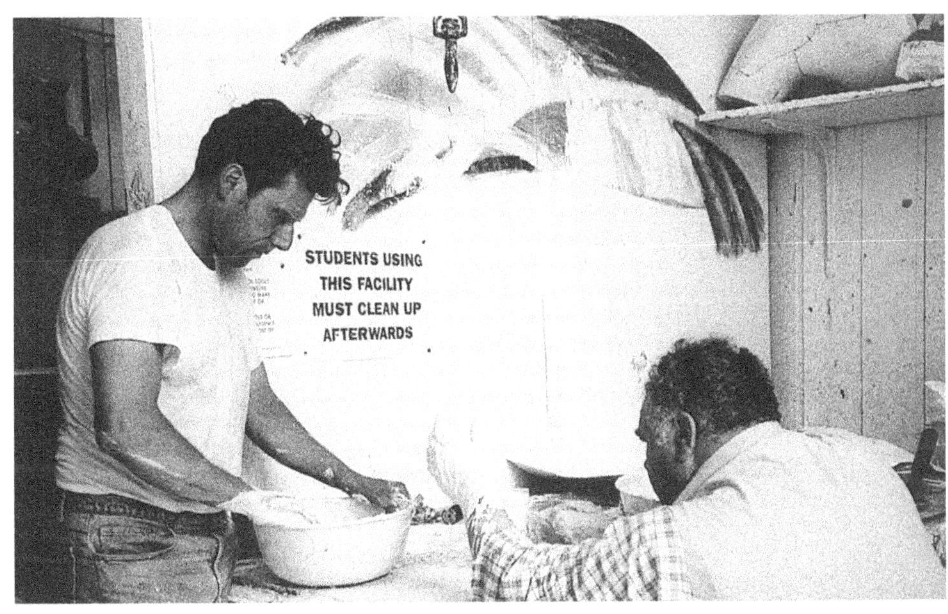
STUDENTS USING
THIS FACILITY
MUST CLEAN UP
AFTERWARDS

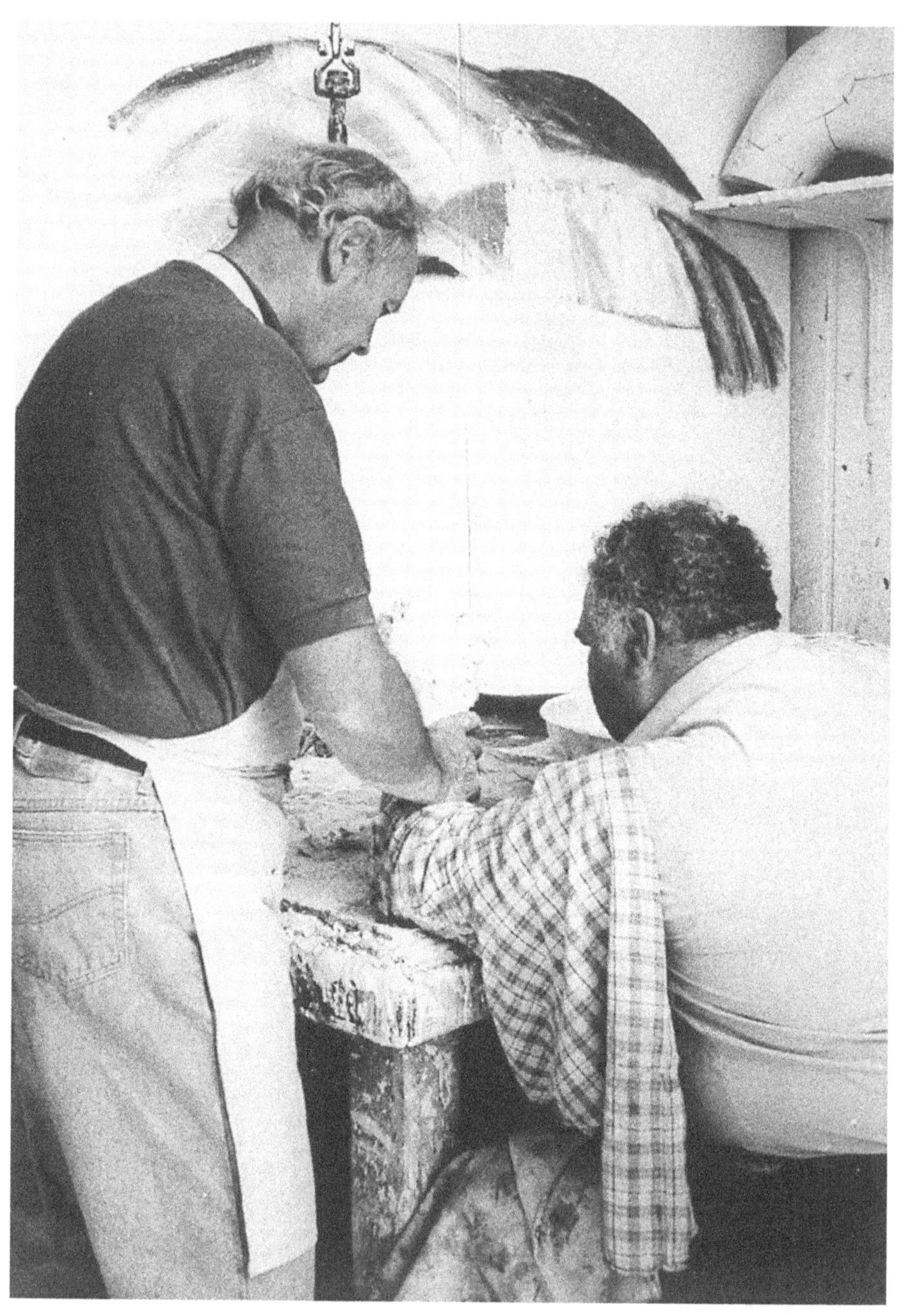

as an artist he knows he has to work with them in the art world.

He refuses to be tied in any way; that much we have learnt. We are left to do our own thing and that suits me. Here we are with the entire facilities of Edinburgh College of Art at our disposal, plus the presence of Paolozzi. Who could want for anything more? It's like being let loose in a sweet shop.

Earlier he had suggested we visit the library and read up about him. I do so and I begin to plough through swathes of material. He has not written anything himself, but plenty of art historians, critics and journalists have. A favourite quotation of his keeps recurring in a number of books and catalogues: "*All human experience is one big collage.*"

Another repeated theme is that his work is infused with a fascination for popular culture as well as modern industrial technology. Not surprisingly he chose to portray himself in his self-portrait "The Artist as Hephaestus", as the Greek god of fire and metal-working – an able metal-worker, a figure known for his creative ability, cunning (though he could be crafty), volatile and vindictive. The work, created in 1987, depicting a standing human figure 2.64 metres (8ft 8in) tall, was commissioned for an office building in High Holborn, London. It's now in a private collection. Paolozzi's interpretation of him combines the artist as man, machine and myth.

At the core of Paolozzi's art lies the ambiguous magic of the *objet trouvé* and the 'ready-mades', the transmutation of quite ordinary objects into something strange, compelling and wonderful. Paolozzi sees the studio as a kitchen: the ingredients are for the most part commonplace, familiar, unexceptional. The kind of stuff, in fact, you could find in a junk shop.

While Kurt Schwitters' collages were transitory, almost with a built-in death wish, Paolozzi seeks to dominate his material and to make a considered and lasting statement, in an essentially traditional way. Paolozzi says that art for him is a lively process, rather than a professional activity.

He says he learnt nothing at the Slade and the remoteness of the staff taught him self-reliance; that as an artist he was on his own. He spent most of his time drawing at the Science Museum and the Natural History Museum, and these studies found echoes in his work during the next five years.

Day Four

"Drawing is as important as you want it to be."

- *Paolozzi*

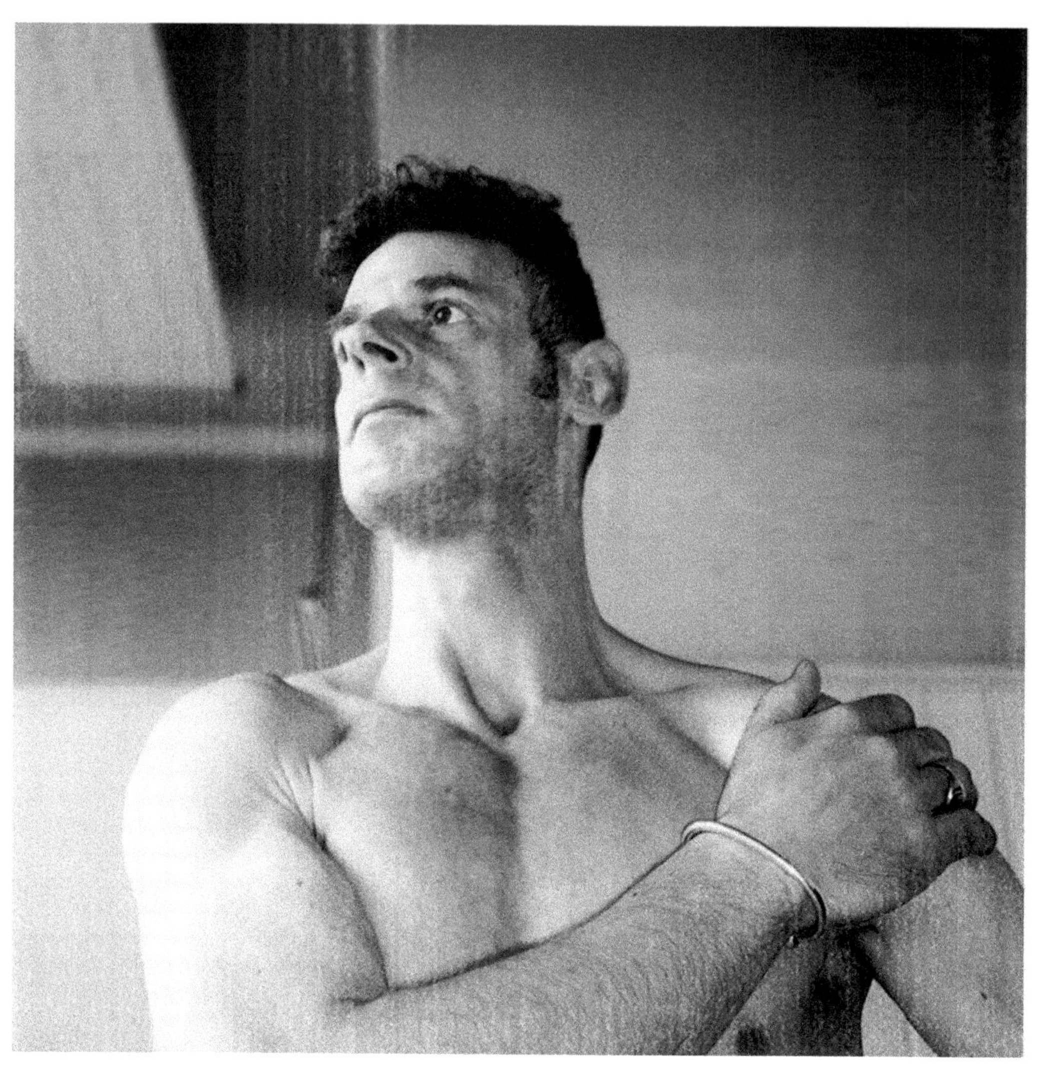

Life class with male model.

Today we discuss drawing. How important is it? We put this question to Paolozzi. He is evasive: "Drawing is as important as you want it to be. You can do anything." Thanks, we had been hoping for clearer guidelines but it is becoming obvious that is not his style.

Here we are on the brink of technology revolutionizing the way art is created and consumed, and many colleges, in fact all the English art schools, have abandoned Life Drawing. But Scotland still retains it as part of the curriculum, albeit in decreasing importance.

However, today has been set aside for Life Drawing with George Donald, and our model is Francis, a male model. He's skinny. I dislike thin models. Fat models are easier to draw.

Still, we are where we are, and I immerse myself in creating big charcoal drawings, and I am glad of my time attending evening classes at Glasgow School of Art.

It soon becomes clear that some of the other students, from 'south of the border', with their neat little pencil drawings, have little if any experience of Life Drawing.

Michael, a graduate of Glasgow School of Art, tackles the project with gusto and panache and his drawings soon evoke admiring glances from the rest of the class.

A young Australian girl, a graduate of Sydney University in Fine Art, had never had a drawing lesson in her life, and another student from Chelsea College of Art said they had abandoned drawing from life years ago.

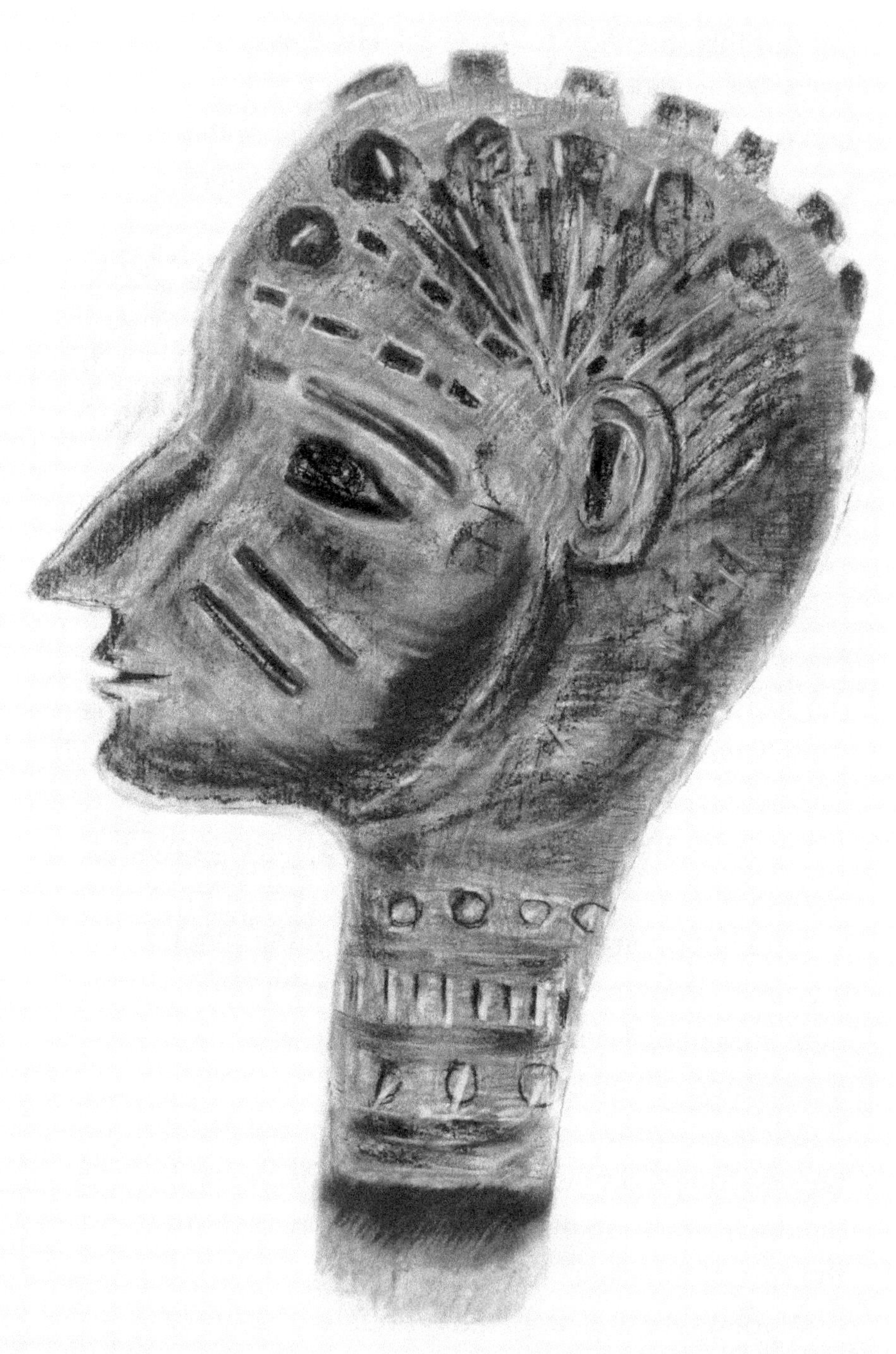

Later that drawing of Francis was to become the basis of my sculpture ....

George Donald tutors our group. He says: "The quality of the drawing depends on how good a conversation you have with yourself, how well you analyse the information in front of you."

Later that drawing of Francis was to become the basis of my sculpture, which owes more than a passing nod to both Giacometti and Paolozzi. I title it: "In the land of the blind the one-eyed man is King," a statement attributed to Desiderius Gerhard Erasmus, Dutch scholar (1465-1536).

Paolozzi has torn up Geraldine's official programme, something she half-expected. Each day is a new beginning, as much of a mystery to her as to the rest of us. Paolozzi hands out catalogues from his recent Munich exhibition, which mention his teaching methods. The writer says: "It is difficult to describe his style of teaching, which is very unobtrusive. No one can resist his charm. Suddenly you realise that you, too, are living and thinking under the spell of his work. He rarely lectures or delivers papers. But the rare exceptions to this rule are occasions to treasure."

He goes on to say "Eduardo himself has remained a child in the positive sense, by retaining all the faculties that most of us lose in adulthood. Curiosity, openness and lack of inhibition, spontaneity and intensity, the ability to look at things as if he were seeing them for the very first time, and to recast the world in his own imagination: these are the main features that characterize him and his work."

Day Five

“There has emerged in Paolozzi a new willingness to treat our whole culture as if it were art.”

- Lawrence Alloway, art critic

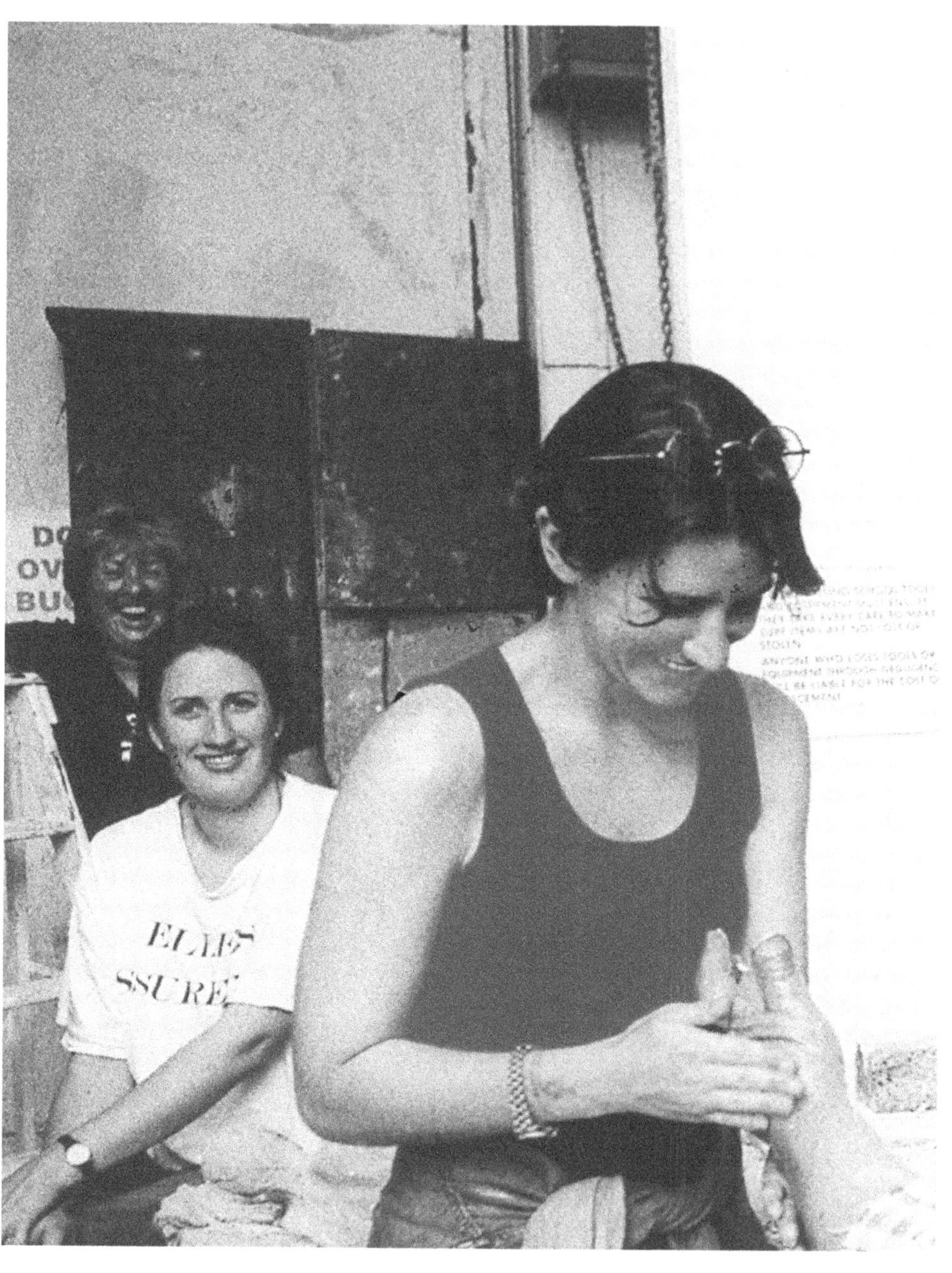

...to see if there could be a little more guidance, some instruction on 'how to be an artist/sculptor'.

There are rumblings of discontent in the studios. Some feel they are not getting their money's worth and one woman is thinking of not coming back after the weekend. "It's a waste of time. I have learnt nothing. I could be in my own studio back home."

She is not alone. We call an emergency studio meeting and we make a group decision to send in the two young girls in our class, (Paolozzi has an eye for pretty women), to ask them to raise the matter with Paolozzi on Monday morning to see if there could be a little more guidance, some instruction on 'how to be an artist/sculptor'. The girls, not surprisingly, are reluctant but peer pressure from the rest of us forces them to agree.

We have the weekend to think about it, and we all leave satisfied at least that something will be done for the second week. But I have a sneaking suspicion that nothing will happen. It's just not his style.

Already he has vetoed a request from one television company and two newspapers wanting to come in and interview us working with Paolozzi. We are disappointed. We reckon it would have been fun. But no, Paolozzi made it clear to Geraldine and George that he was having none of it.

So the media are banned. The college is annoyed. Here would be a golden opportunity to promote Edinburgh College of Art, to record an historic art event and it is closed to the outside world. After all, a Masterclass with Paolozzi is

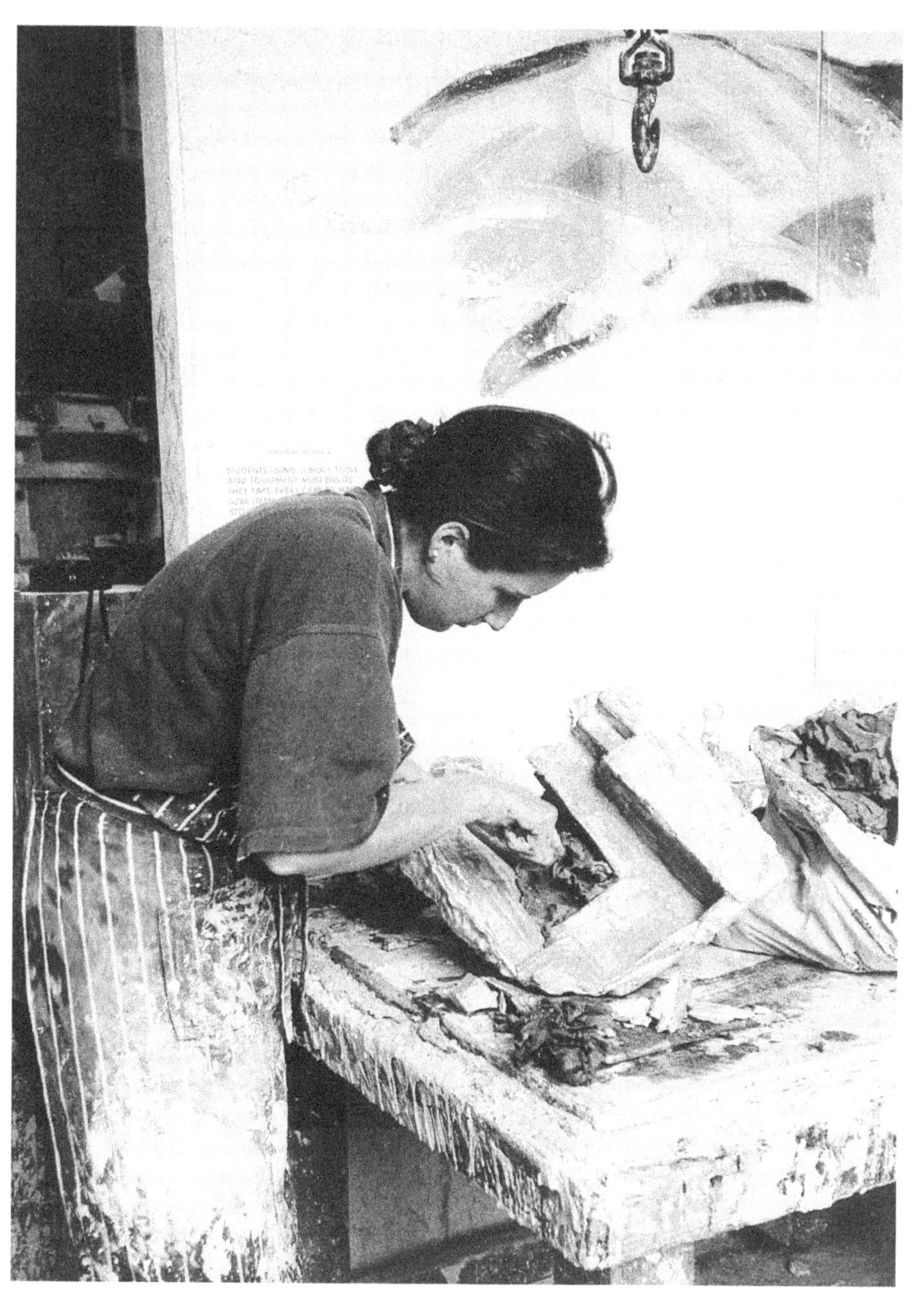

Students are engrossed in their own creative process.

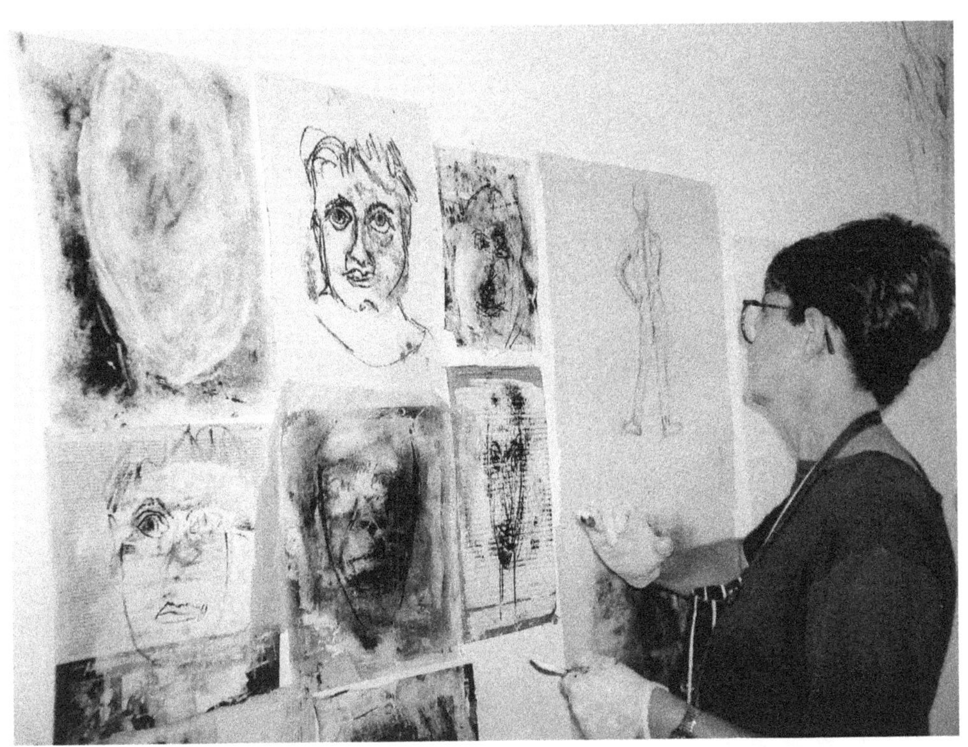

Despite, or maybe because of, the lack of formal instruction we do learn and at the end of the first week I take stock of what I have learnt.

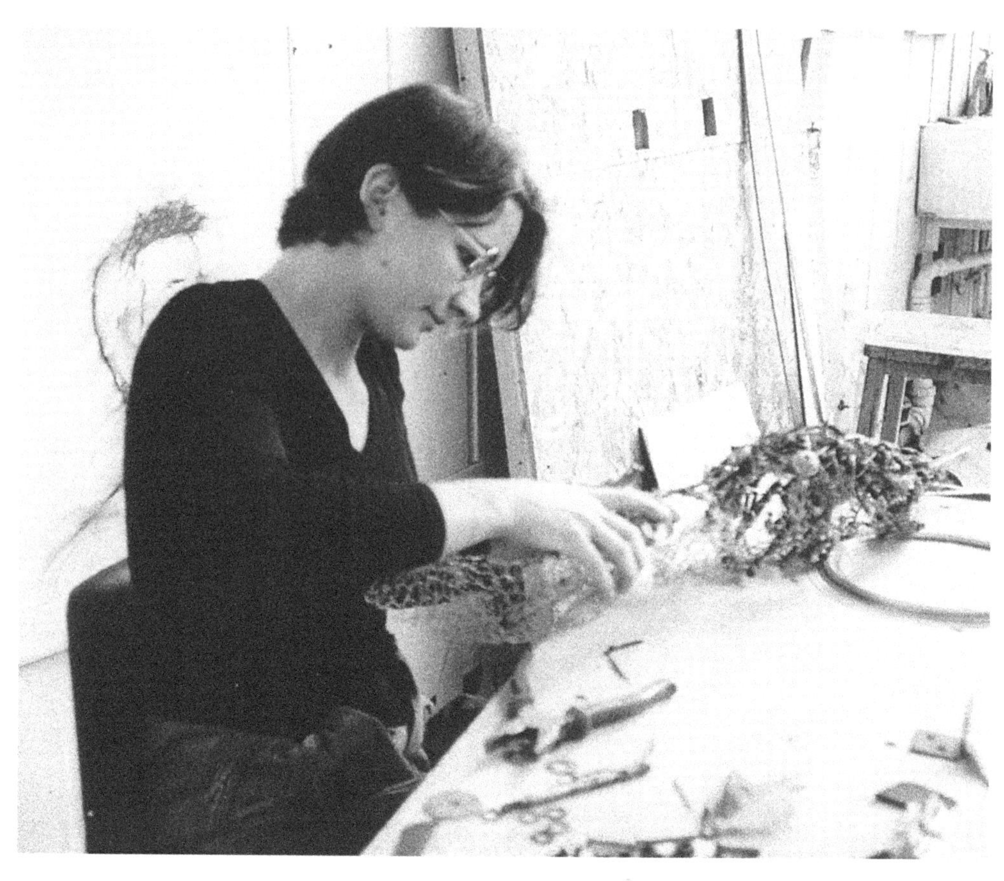

A delicate moment calling for combined craft skills with aesthetic judgement.

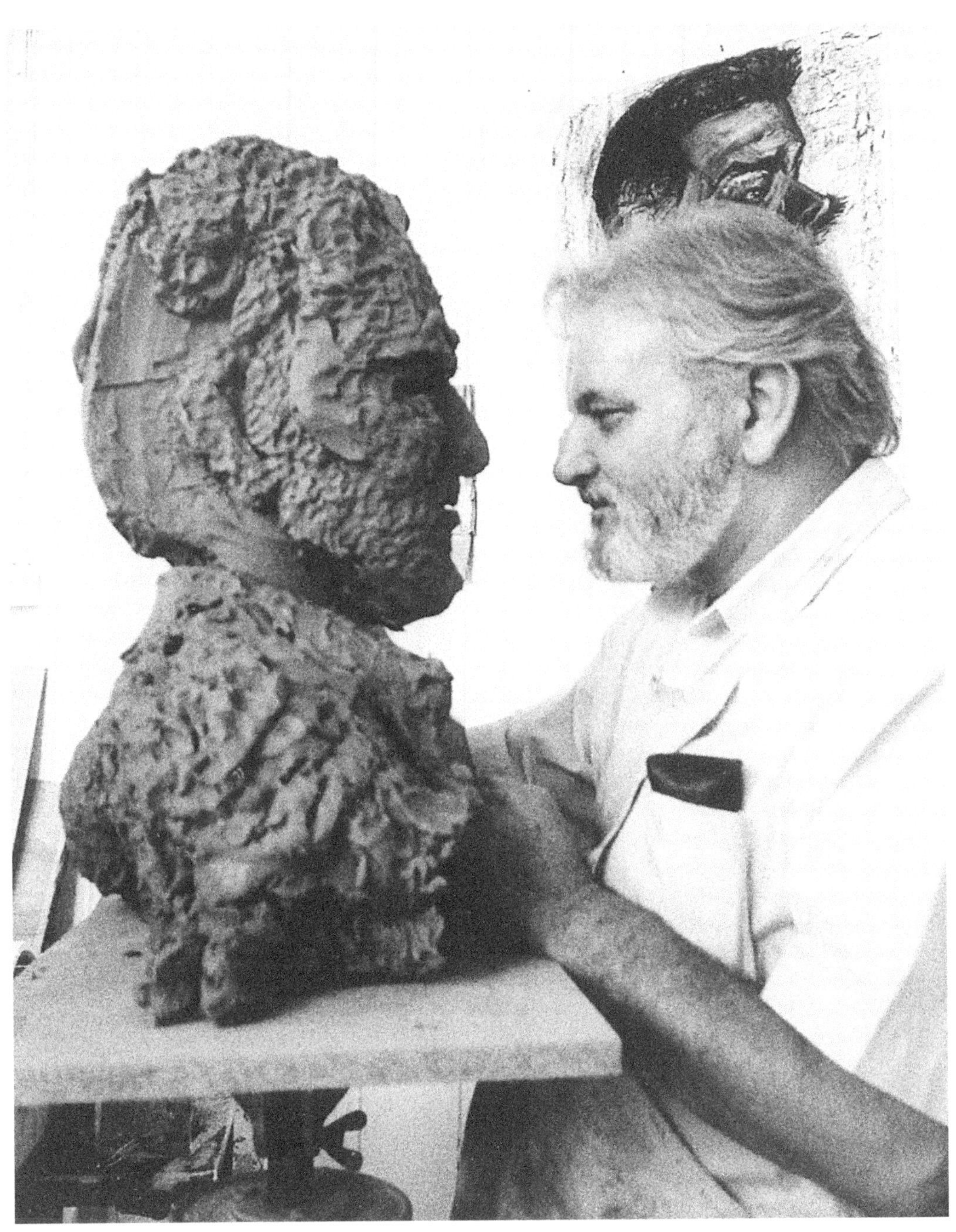

One student adds the finishing touch to this self-portrait.

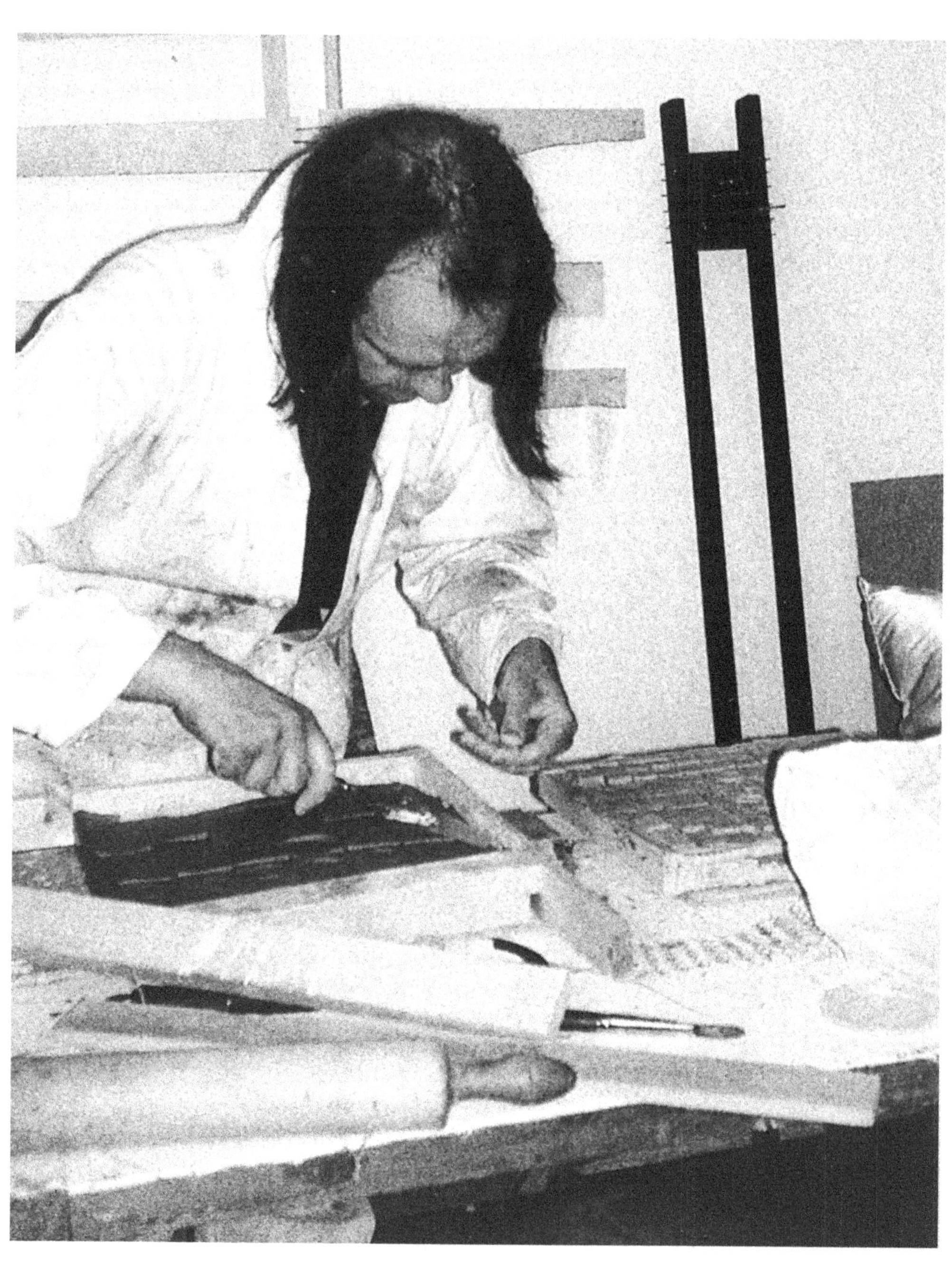

This young printmaker shows patience, skill and dexterity as he creates huge wall hangings.

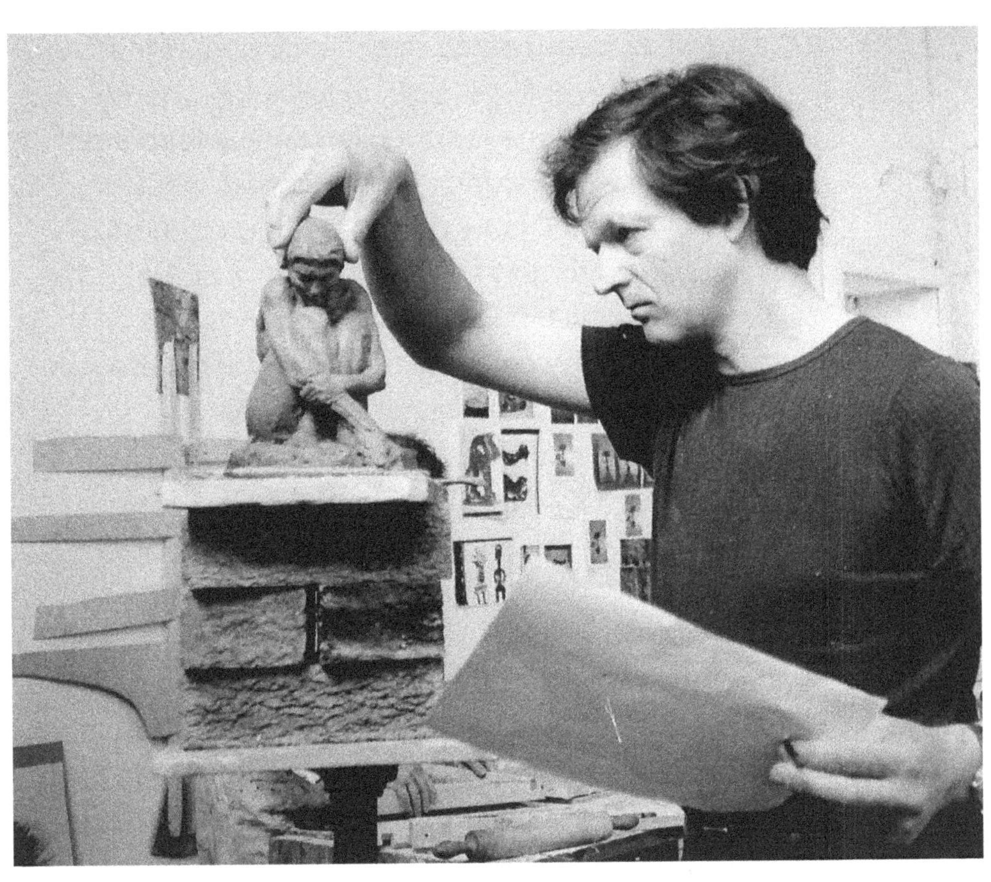

Just checking. This figurative sculptor makes some last minute adjustments.

a never-to-be-repeated experience and all that kudos for the college is going to be lost. He will not allow even one reporter, let alone a television camera, into the studio. I am uncertain whether he knows I am a journalist about to give up daily newspapers to go to Glasgow School of Art. I suspect even if he knows he does not care because he has not shown the slightest interest in any of us either as artists or individuals.

Nevertheless, it was Paolozzi himself who ordered us all to keep a diary and he would read them at the end. Despite, or maybe because of, the lack of formal instruction we do learn and at the end of the first week I take stock of what I have learnt. Some say you learn as much as 50 per cent from other students in a group situation as you would from your teacher. (Maybe more in the case of Paolozzi....)

Gavin, the young printmaker from the Royal College of Art laboured all week on a series of woodcuts, six foot panels, from which he takes silk prints creating beautiful fragile wall hangings.

I cannot fail to be impressed with his skill, dedication, hard work and tenacity. Do I have what it takes to be an artist? For the first time I get a glimpse into what serious studio work is all about, the long hours, the attention to detail, the perseverance to keep going when things start to go wrong.

There are others too in the studio from whom I learn. Vince from Malta gives me the name of a software package which allows me to create

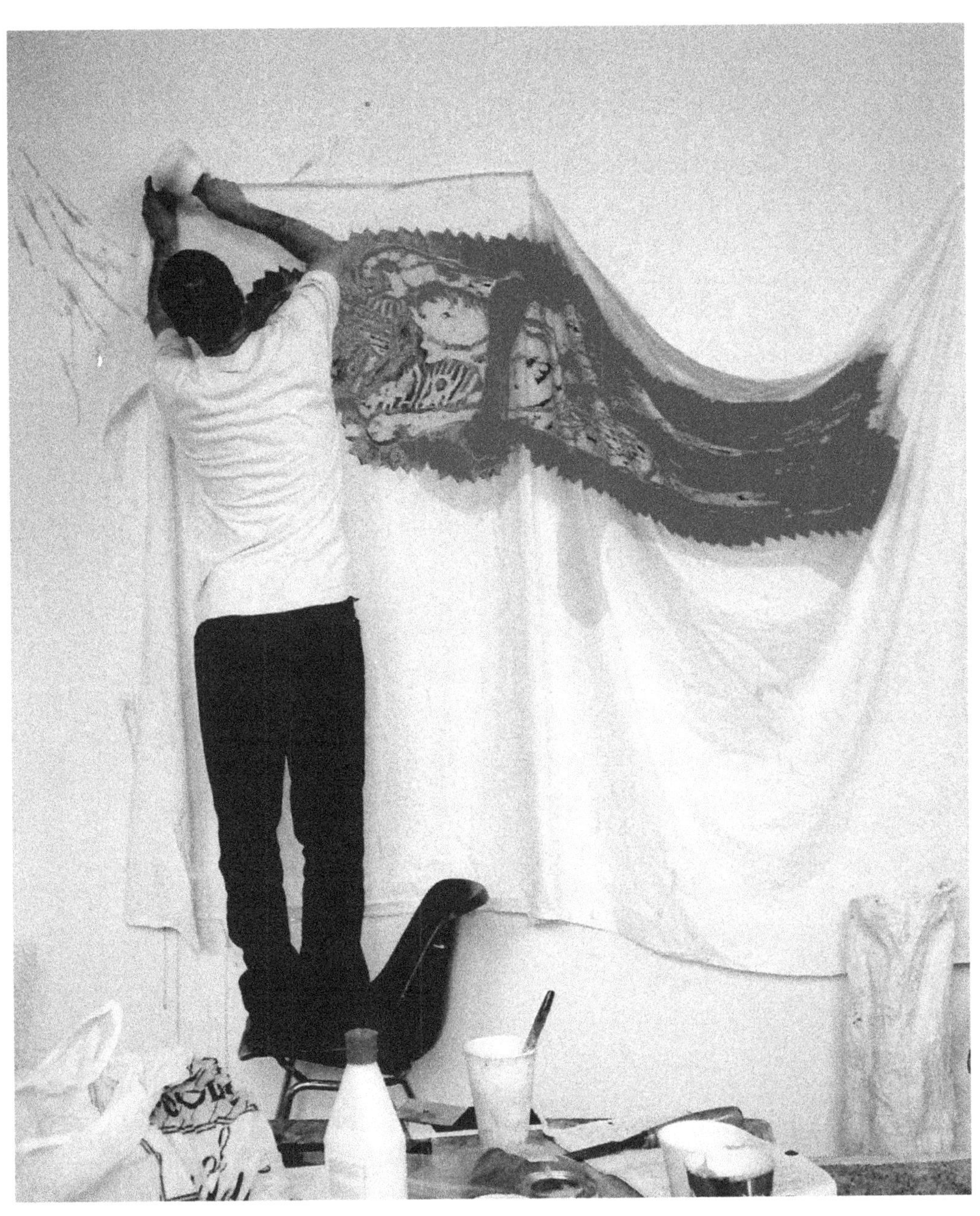

Gavin, the young printmaker from the Royal College of Art, laboured all week on a series of woodcuts, six-foot panels, from which he takes silk prints creating beautiful fragile wall hangings.

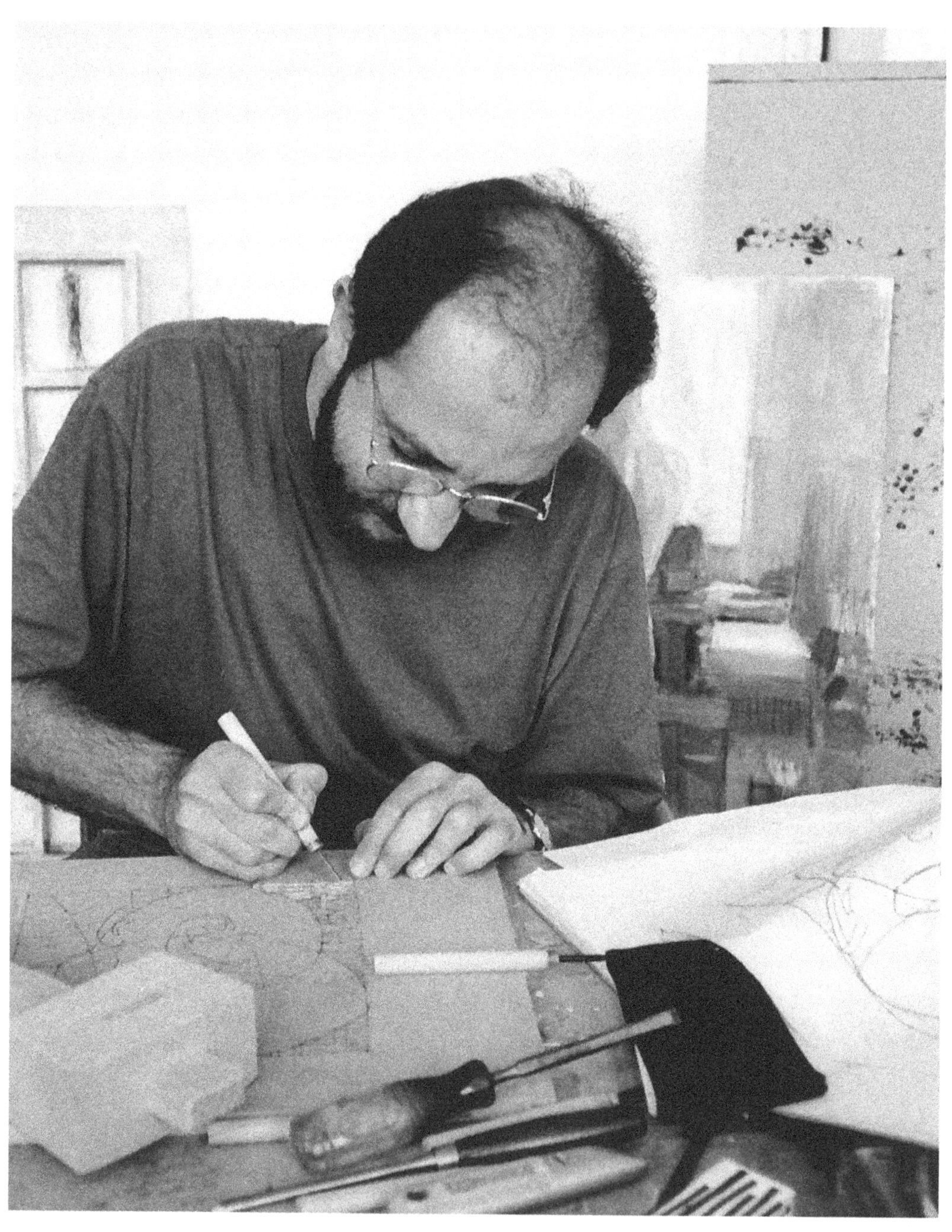

There are others too in the studio from whom I learn. Vince from Malta gives me the name of a software package ...

inter-active CD Roms and Martin, the orthopaedic surgeon, has revealed a whole new world of potential castings - packages used for medical supplies.

And Paolozzi? Well, on a practical level he urged me to photograph my work, something I only did occasionally but not as an art form in itself. That's on a practical level, but much more important has been the intellectual contact with a mind like his. What he calls osmosis, difficult to define but something has happened. One begins to see the world through his eyes. He has taught us to plunder the past, to ransack other cultures for images and to re-interpret them in our own visual language. He gives one freedom to find oneself or, as he says, "Follow your own obsessions". His presence alone gives out a certain physical as well as intellectual ambience.

Paolozzi has finally set us a project: create a self-portrait. I tackle this with gusto. I am going to make a sculpture using chicken wire and plaster. And it's life-size, thanks to Paolozzi. He happened to be passing the corridor where I worked – the piece was too big to go in the studio with so many other people already there, so I thought 'why not move myself into the corridor?' So I did.

Paolozzi saw it. "Make it big … if you get stuck I will give you a hand."

The thought petrifies me. By late afternoon I have finished my wire construction. Some suggest I leave it just as it is and that I would ruin it by covering it in plaster.

Of course I do not listen to advice. The problem is I have set my mind on plastering.

George asks me to become the official photographer for the course, which simply gives me permission to keep on clicking. But I don't think Paolozzi liked the pictures I took of him having his hands cast. He asked why they were so dark. A member of the course rushed to my defence: "She is on a sculpture course, not a photography course."

At the end of the day we go to the Scottish Gallery of Modern Art in Edinburgh to see the Giacometti exhibition, which is staying open for a few extra hours to accommodate us. I arrive late, with another student, in my red sports car. I park outside the gallery, only to see the disapproving look on Paolozzi's face, as he stands on the lawn with a cluster of students around him.

I suddenly become aware that my flashy car is more bling, Glasgow and the world of journalism than the cultured art world of Edinburgh, which disapproves of showy statements.

We hope for some words of wisdom from Paolozzi, some insight into Alberto Giacometti's working process or snippets of gossip from his personal life.

There is none.

An odd incident occurs later while we are in the gallery. We are standing looking at the work of Giacometti when I become aware of Paolozzi staring intently at me. Then he walks out into the garden and sits down on a bench, surrounded by his own sculptures. I follow, and for a few minutes he talks about his work, the way it has survived the elements – it's bronze – and the way it is placed in the garden. We sit in silence contemplating the sculptures. He wants to share it with me and I feel honoured.

Day Six

“Paolozzi sees the studio as a sort of kitchen.”

- Michael Middleton, art historian

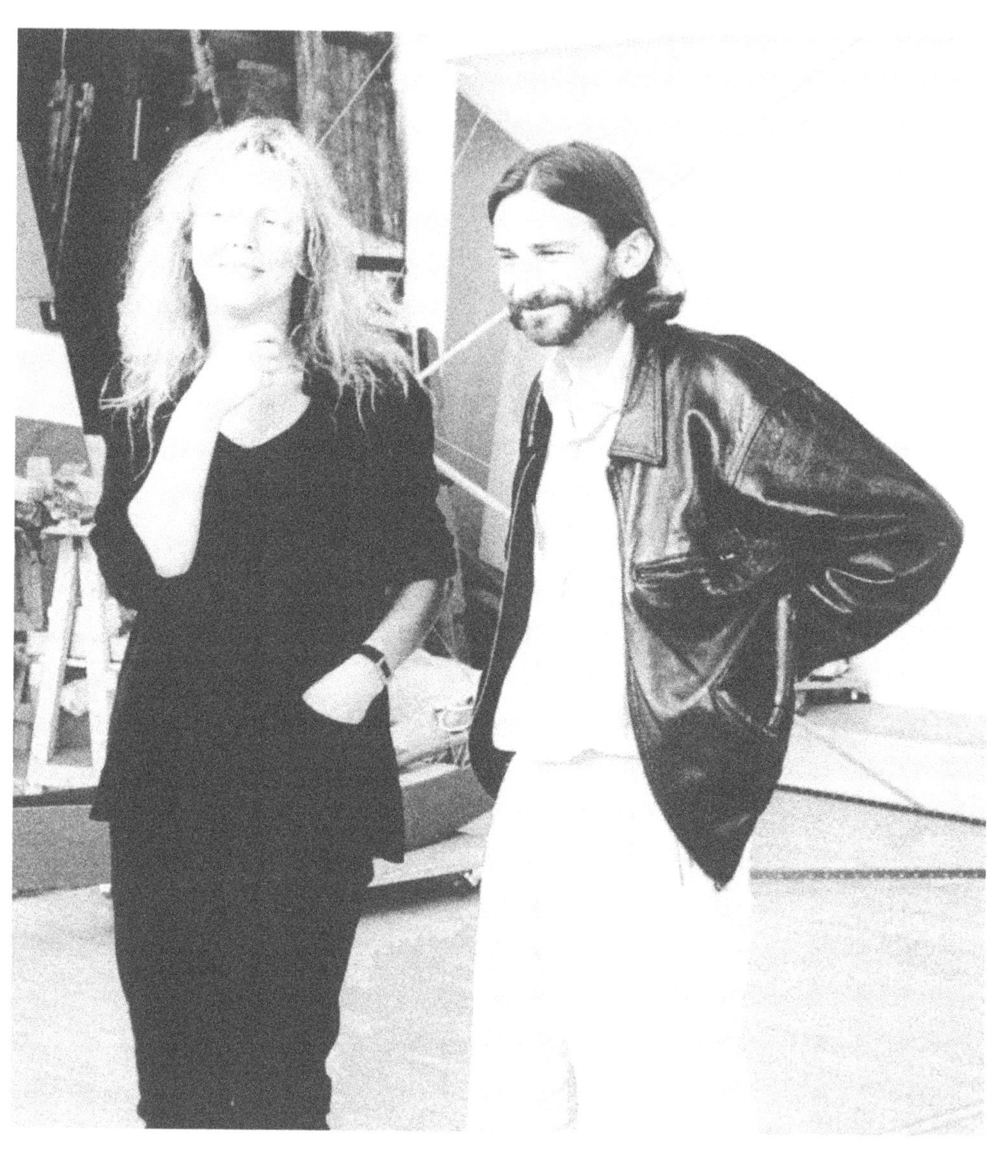

Artist Elizabeth Ogilivie with printmaker Paul Furneaux

Today we visit Burntisland to draw and photograph in the shipyard. It's the only project Paolozzi had specifically requested to be put on the schedule. I ask Geraldine if Paolozzi will be with us since it would be interesting to see this industrial landscape through his eyes. "Who knows?" says Geraldine raising her eyes skywards. He has already torn up her timetable.

I am dithering about going. After all I am keen to get on with my self-portrait and I can go to the Fife coast any day. Most people have already left, sharing transport. Paolozzi asks if I am going. It suddenly occurs to me that he might want a lift.

Should I offer? Then a thought occurs to me. How would the bulky form of Paolozzi squeeze into my tiny sports car? Would the seat belt go around him? Think of the embarrassment! Better not to risk it.

"I think I will stay and work in the studio," I murmur and move away. Geraldine comes into the studio. "Ah there you are! I am looking for someone to deliver a bottle of champagne to Bob Callender and Elizabeth Ogilvie. You will all be ending up there after a day sketching. George forgot to take it with him. You are going, aren't you?"

So that decided it. I would go and sketch. And Paolozzi stays in the studio with the three young girls who announce that they too are staying. (He attracts young women like bees to a honeypot.)

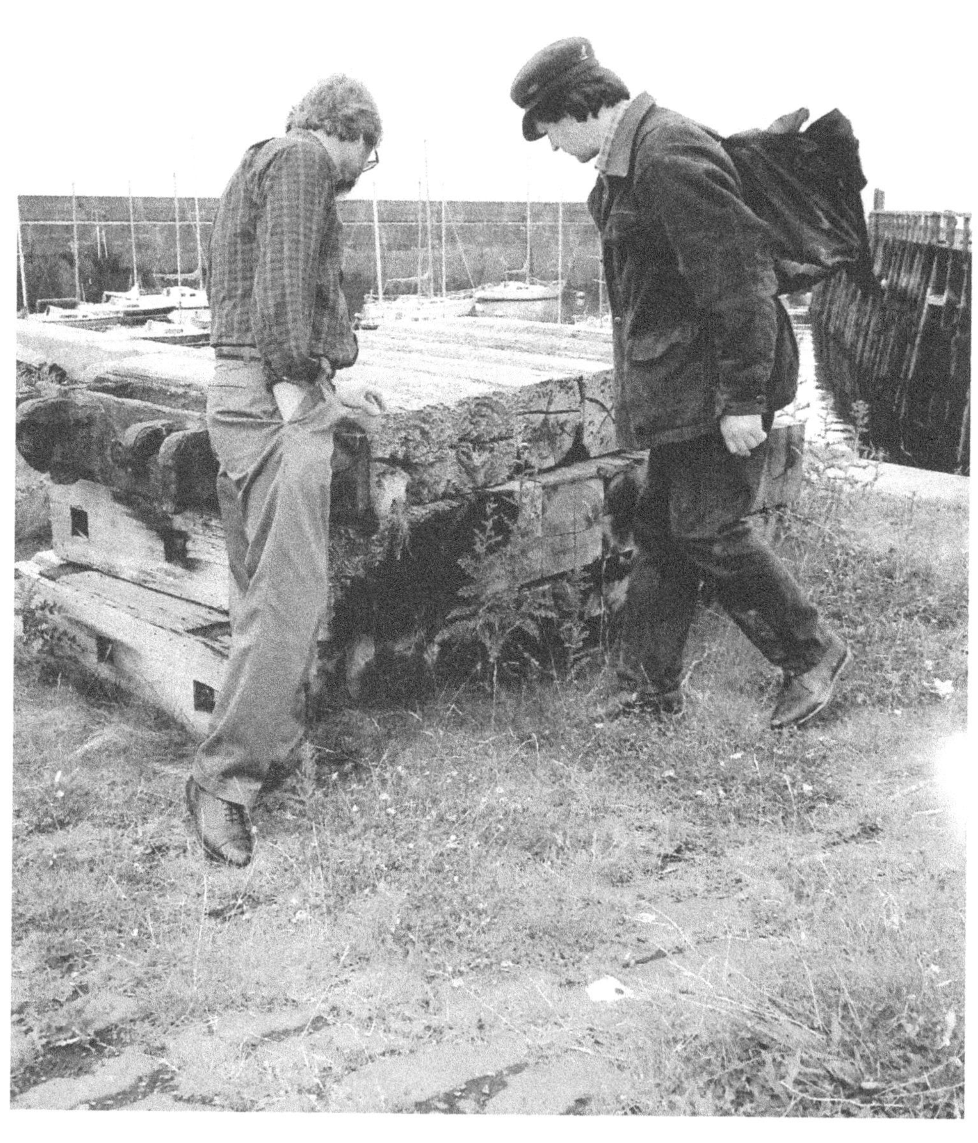

George Donald (left) touring shipyard with a Masterclass student.

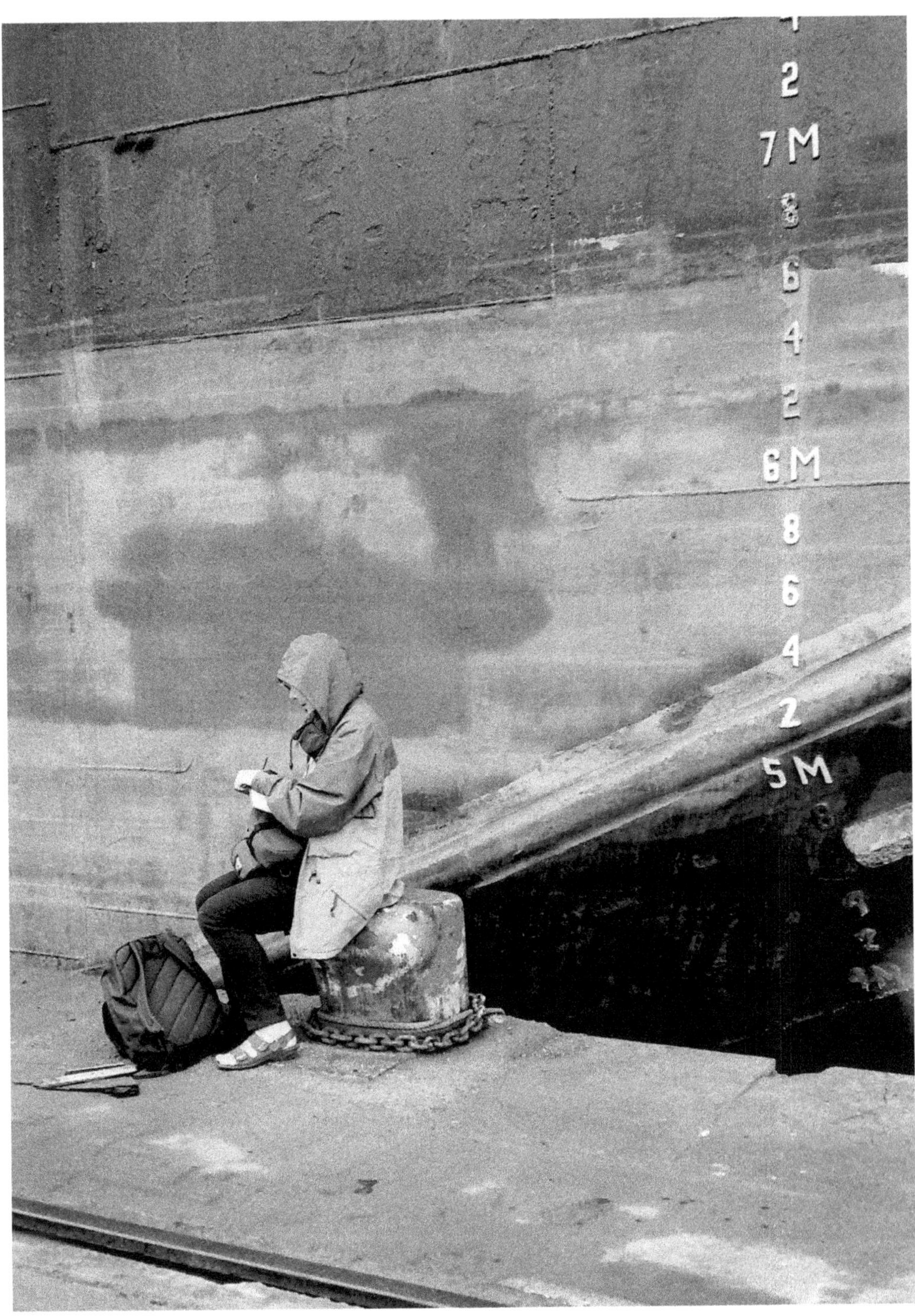

Student sketching.

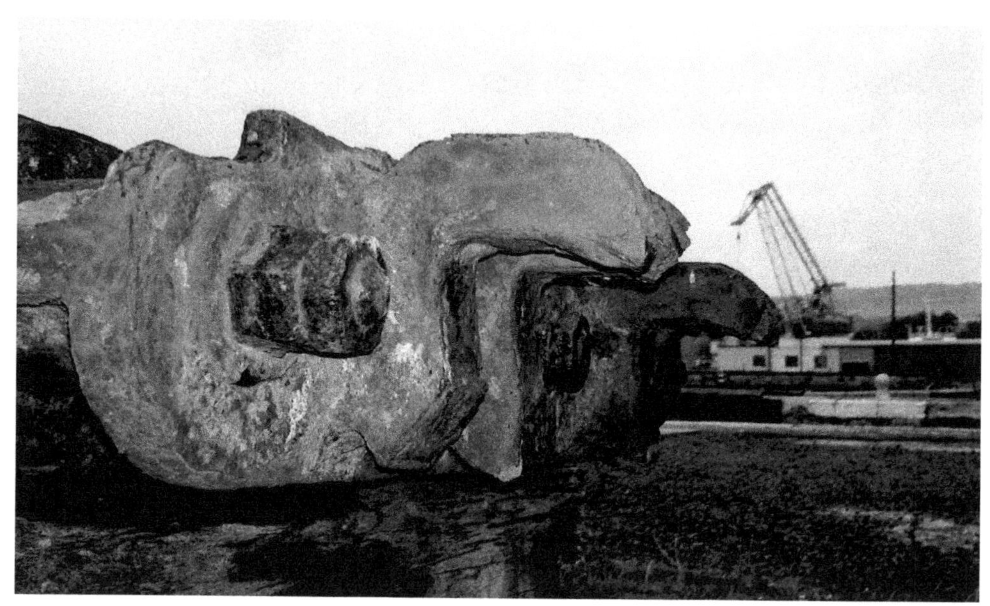

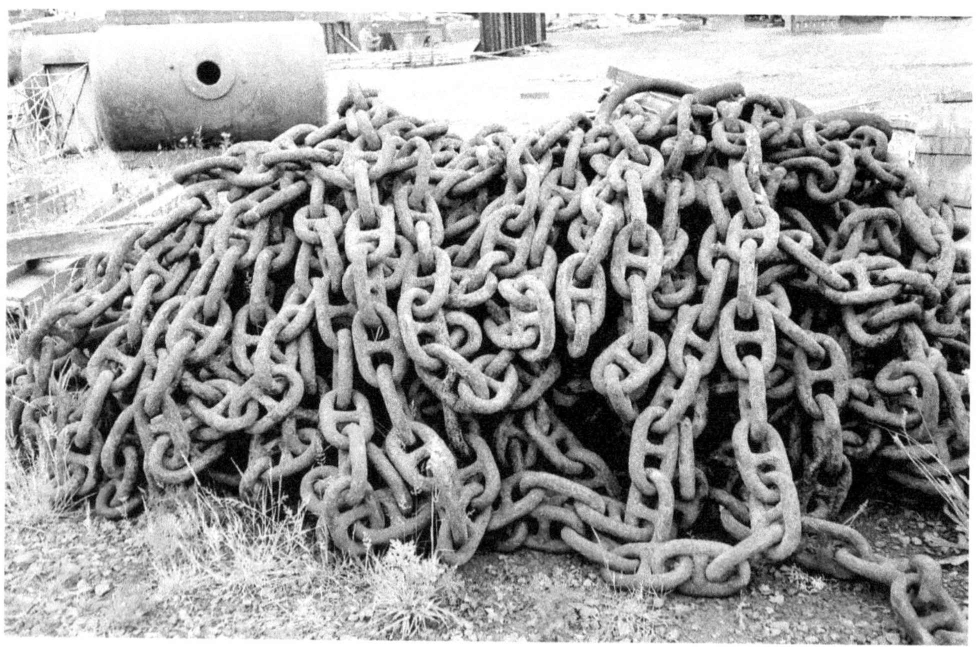

I began to see the industrial landscape through his eyes. ...

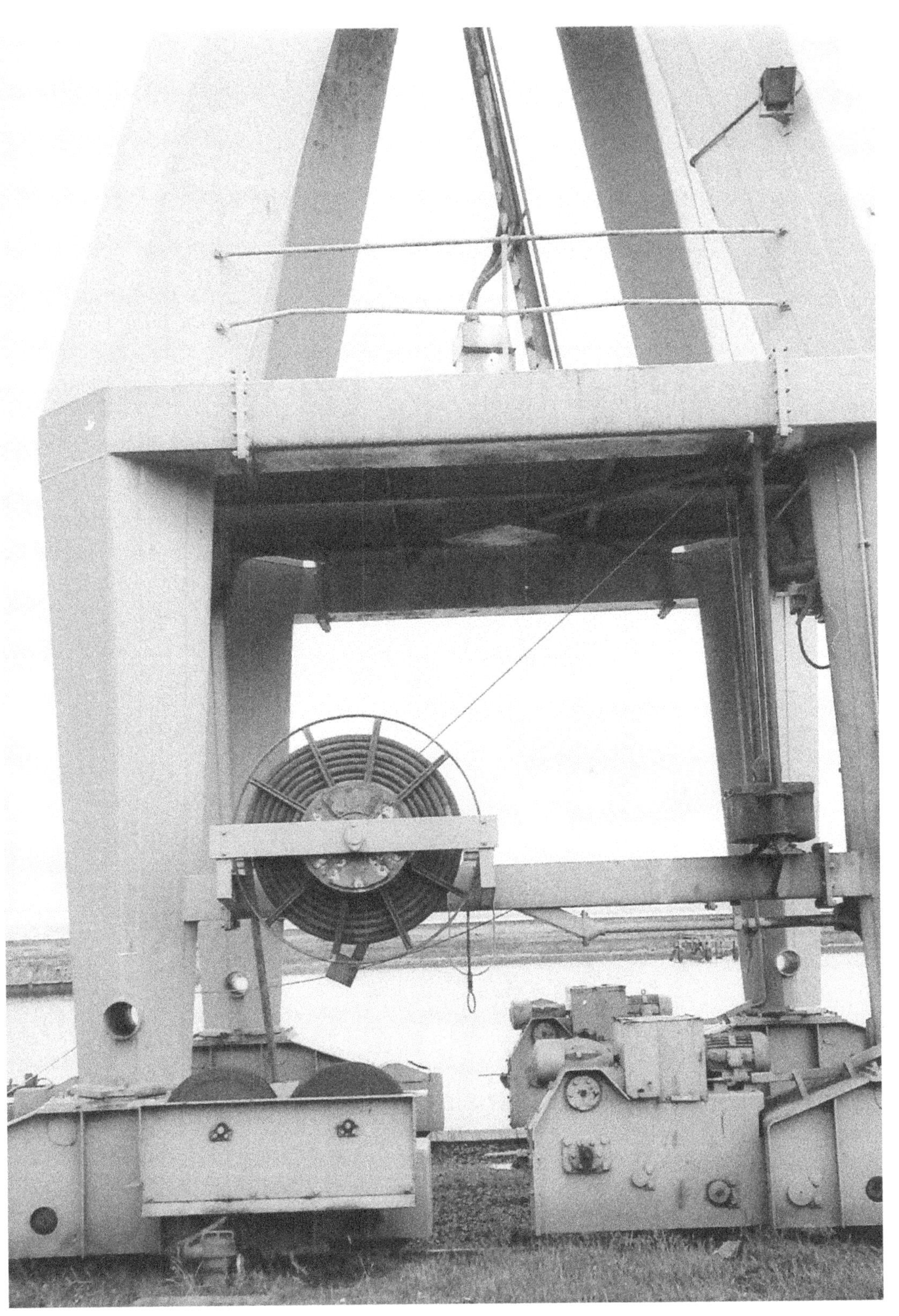

A crane in the Burntisland yard.

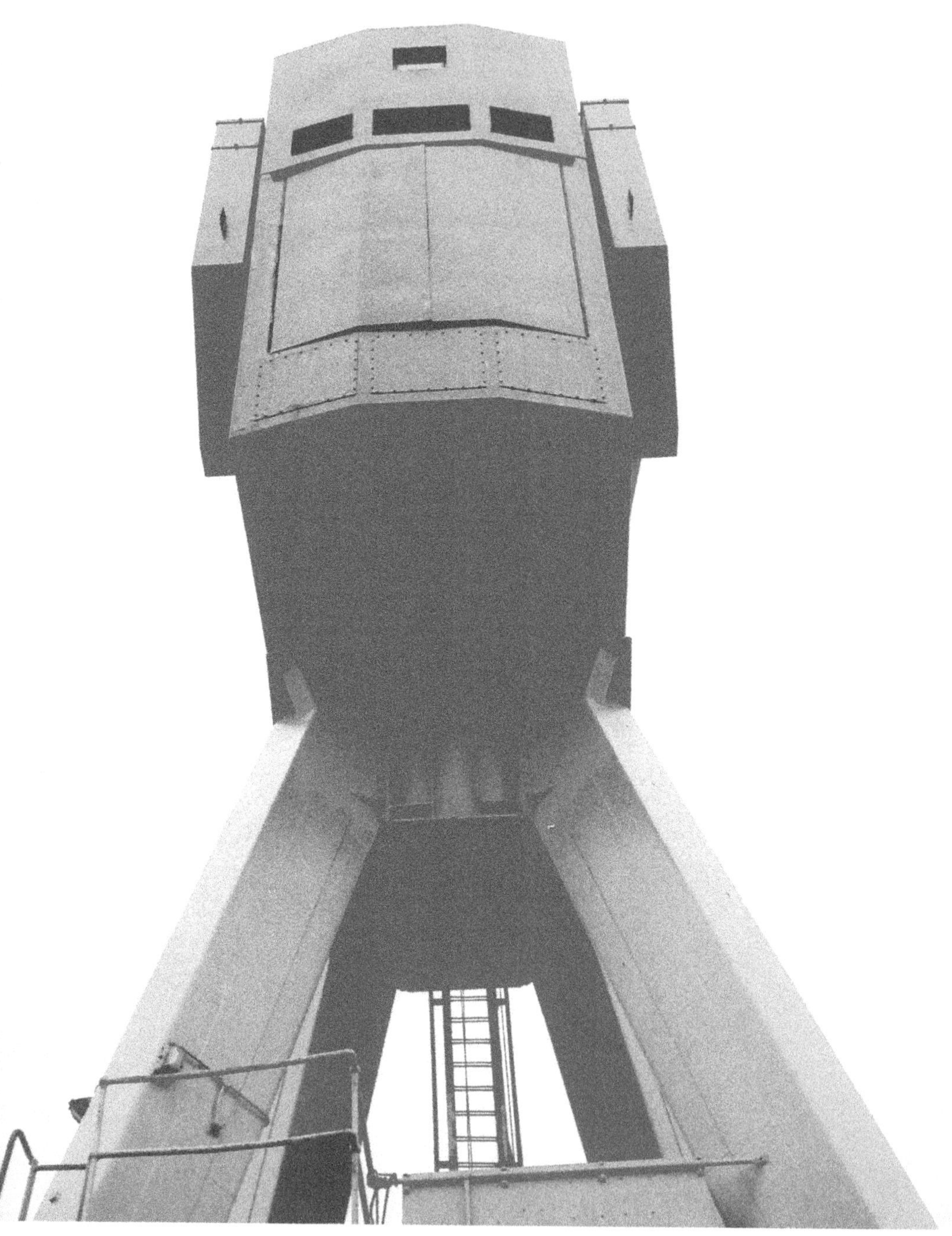

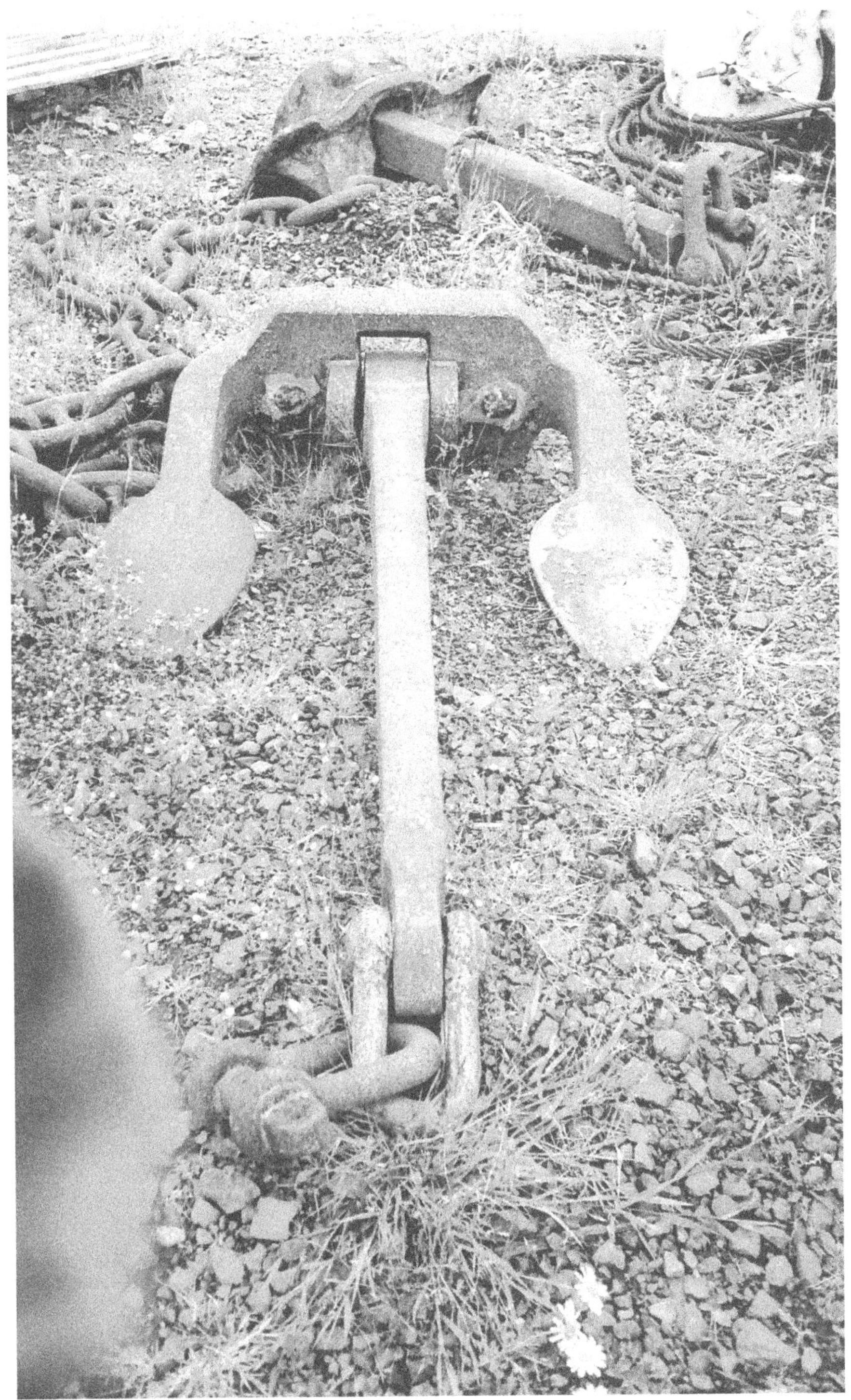

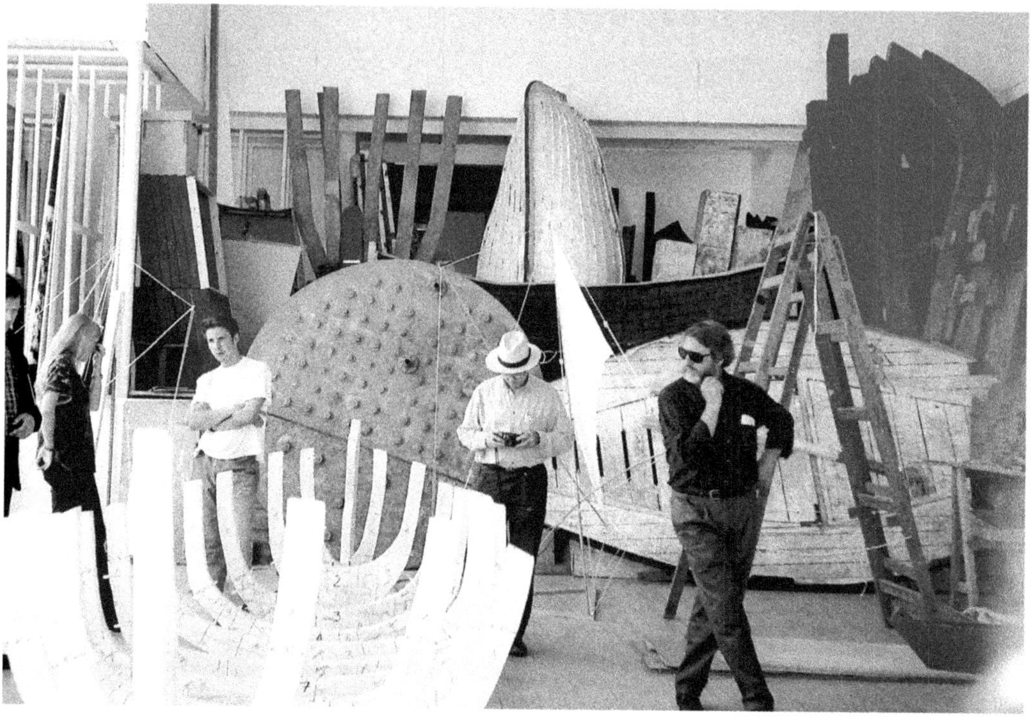

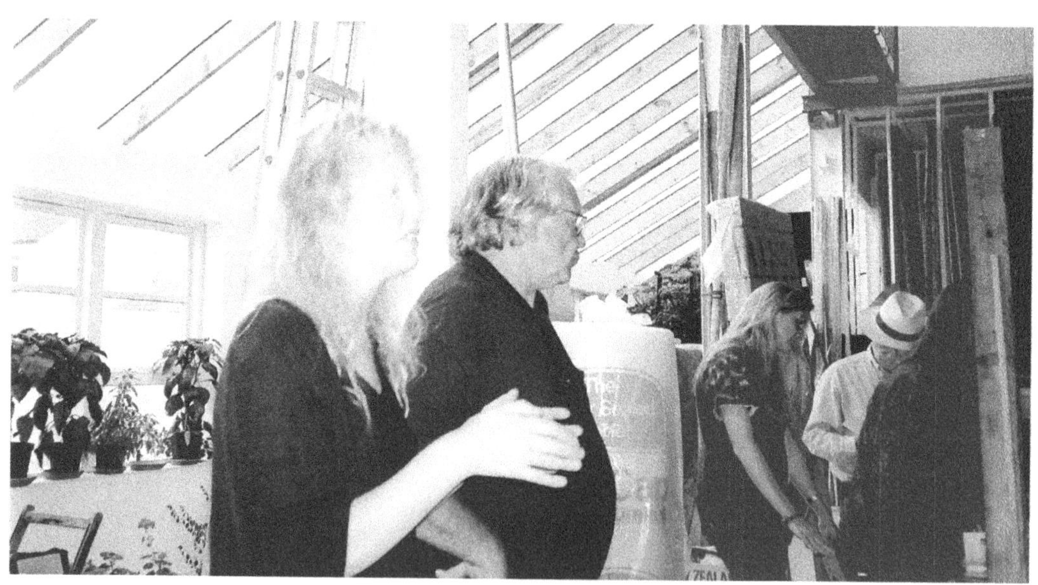

...the studios of artists Elizabeth Ogilvie and Bob Callender in Kinghorn.

Would they tackle him about the studio problems? This would be an excellent opportunity. They do not.

But I am glad I did go on this sketching expedition, because that's when I made a discovery. Even though Paolozzi was not there, his influence had already become so pervasive that I began to see the industrial landscape through his eyes. Huge shipyard cranes metamorphosed before my very eyes into strange robotic creatures. It was as if I had been given a new pair of eyes, a most extraordinary experience.

At the end of the afternoon we meet up in the studios of artists Elizabeth Ogilvie and Bob Callender in Kinghorn. Some years ago they bought a disused cinema and turned it into a series of huge open plan studios with a panoramic view over the Fife coast. I hand over the bottle of champagne. They are disappointed Paolozzi is not with us.

That evening, I pick up a copy of Paolozzi's catalogue of works from Germany. Dr Frank Whitford, writing in the catalogue for the exhibition to celebrate the Goethe Medal Award 1991, says

> Although Paolozzi had been making graphics for many years, it was in Hamburg that he first thought about making a major statement in the medium. The choice of theme – Central European and intellectually demanding – marked a slackening of Paolozzi's interest in America and American popular culture, which had been important during the 1950s, and the growth of a new awareness of his continental roots.

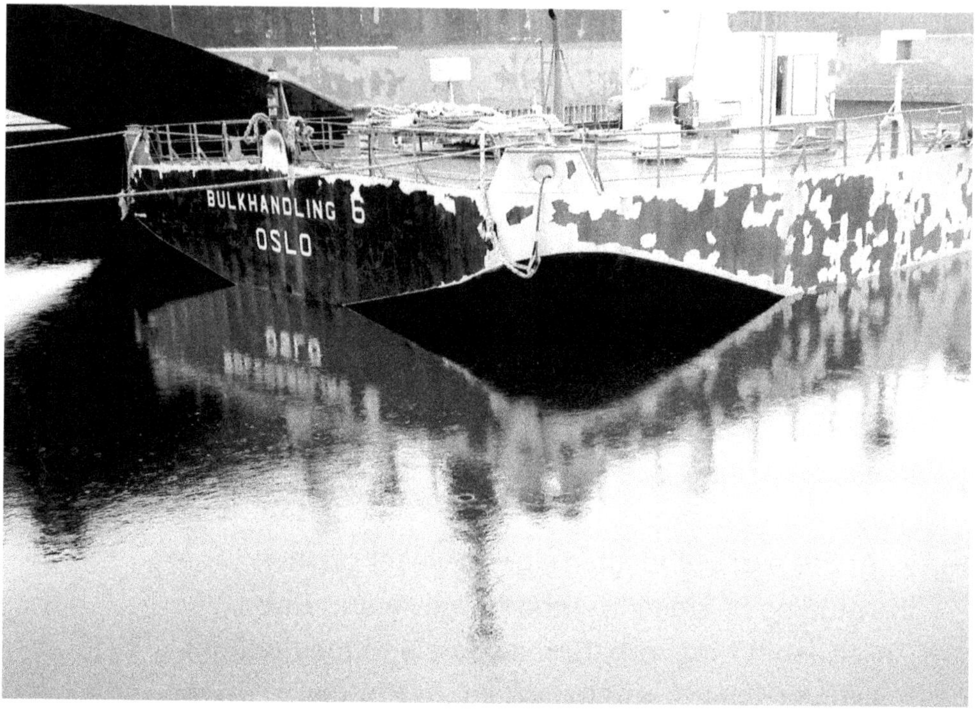

BULKHANDLING 6
OSLO

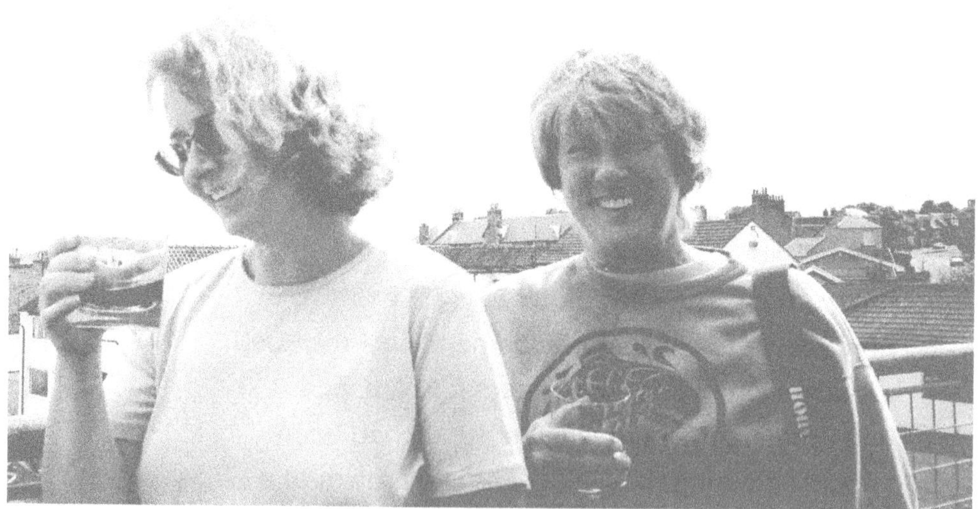

Paolozzi had never found dominant artist attitudes in Britain particularly congenial. They were too concerned with nostalgia and polite taste too. Hostile to the iconoclastic aspects of modernism … In Germany, where the machine aesthetic was invented, he found the optimism and the belief in the benefits of technology invigorating. New ideas were accepted and applied with an almost ruthless consistency unknown in nostalgic Britain.

Day Seven

"Art is not produced in art colleges but in big studios, with people working together."

- Paolozzi

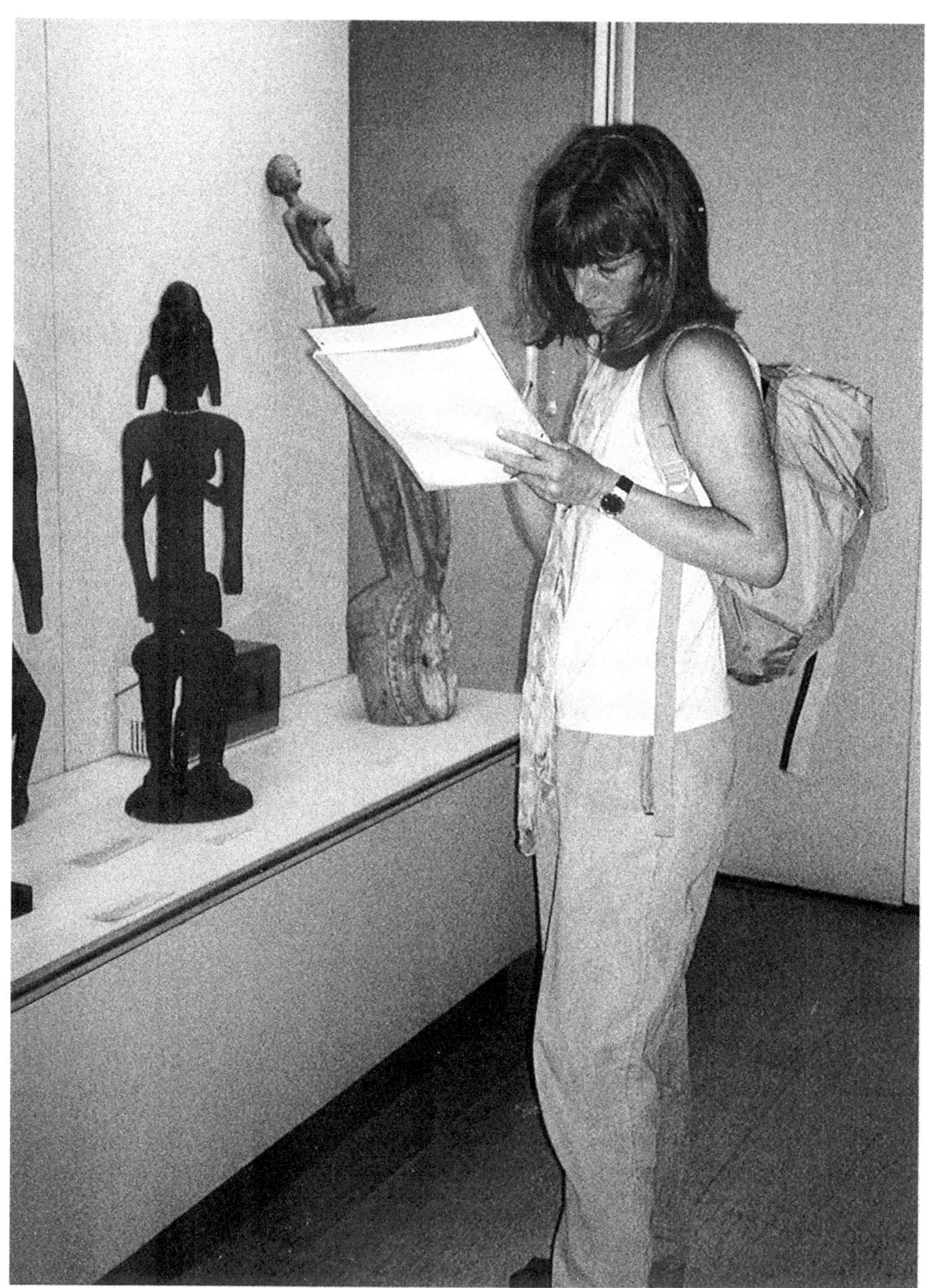

Today Paolozzi talks about his art. “When I left the Slade and went to Paris in 1947, I had a mission to see modern art and in particular Surrealism, and to meet real artists for the first time. They were all still alive and extremely approachable.”

There he met Braque, Arp, Brancusi, Dubuffet, Leger, Giacometti, Miro and Tristan Tzara. “Giacometti was unbelievably amiable. We met twice a week. We didn’t have diaries – we just turned up at the Café Flore or the Deux Magots. We were all there every night,” he recalls. The casual “we” is taken to include not only Sartre and Camus, but also such young Scottish artists as William Gear, William Turnbull and Alan Davie.

“Modern art isn’t easy,” he says. “I remember Freddie Ayer, the philosopher, telling me he found modern art very confusing. He longed for a big book on modern aesthetics so he could look up everything to see if each artist had the right amount of classifications and points. It just doesn’t work that way, does it?”

I spend most of the day in the plaster room. I am covered in the stuff, and exhausted. Late in the afternoon Paolozzi wanders in. “Something to keep you going,” he says to those of us still working and hands out jelly-babies. I grab a few, grateful for the sugar, for the energy surge. He understood how we lose ourselves in the act of creating, how we move into a different zone.

We have finally lost our fear and awe of him and during one of his impromptu lectures we raise a number of issues. Meanwhile the studio rebellion is forgotten because by now we are all too engrossed in our own work.

I ask him what he saw as the purpose of a Masterclass since it was clear that his ideas are very different from ours. His answer surprises us. "To bring you lot together for a start, so that you can learn from each other. That's important."

Something else has also taken place which is much more subtle, difficult to quantify, and more important. He has given us permission to experiment, to be free, to throw out the rule-books of "What is art?"

Some students say they have found the courage to do things they would never have dared do on their own outside the security of such a class. Others are disconcerted by the freedom. They want rules, they want structures, and they want to be told how to become a sculptor. Paolozzi's answer is simple: There are no rules. You find your own salvation.

On a personal level I have revelled in the freedom, finding it exhilarating, never dreaming for a moment that a Paolozzi Masterclass would give me such freedom to rummage through other cultures and plunder them for my own play. Previous classes I have attended have been full of rules which I have tried to follow only to get bored, and I go my own way, usually following a skirmish with a teacher who has tried unsuccessfully to 'reform' me.

During another discussion he explains that the key to his work is geometry. Has he used computers? What does he think of them? This is a touchy subject. The group on the whole is anti-computers and technology, with a couple of exceptions. Another heated argument takes place with people saying it's not 'proper art' because it's made by a machine.

In the midst of this, Paolozzi throws a letter on the table and orders us to read it. It's an invitation to visit Heriot Watt University to look at the way artists and sculptors can use virtual reality.

In the evening we visit the Scottish Museum of Mankind in Edinburgh and receive a lecture from the curator on primitive art. (Paolozzi chides me for not removing all the plaster from my arms. I tell him I can't get the stuff off.)

Later two-thirds of our group returns to the studios to continue working until 9 pm. Undoubtedly something is happening in the group dynamics. We are all wrestling with our personal projects, ideas that refuse to materialize in the way we anticipated. One girl is alarmed that her two-weeks work will result in a failed cast. She doesn't leave until 9 this evening and will be in at 8 am to see Ron, the technician, for some help.

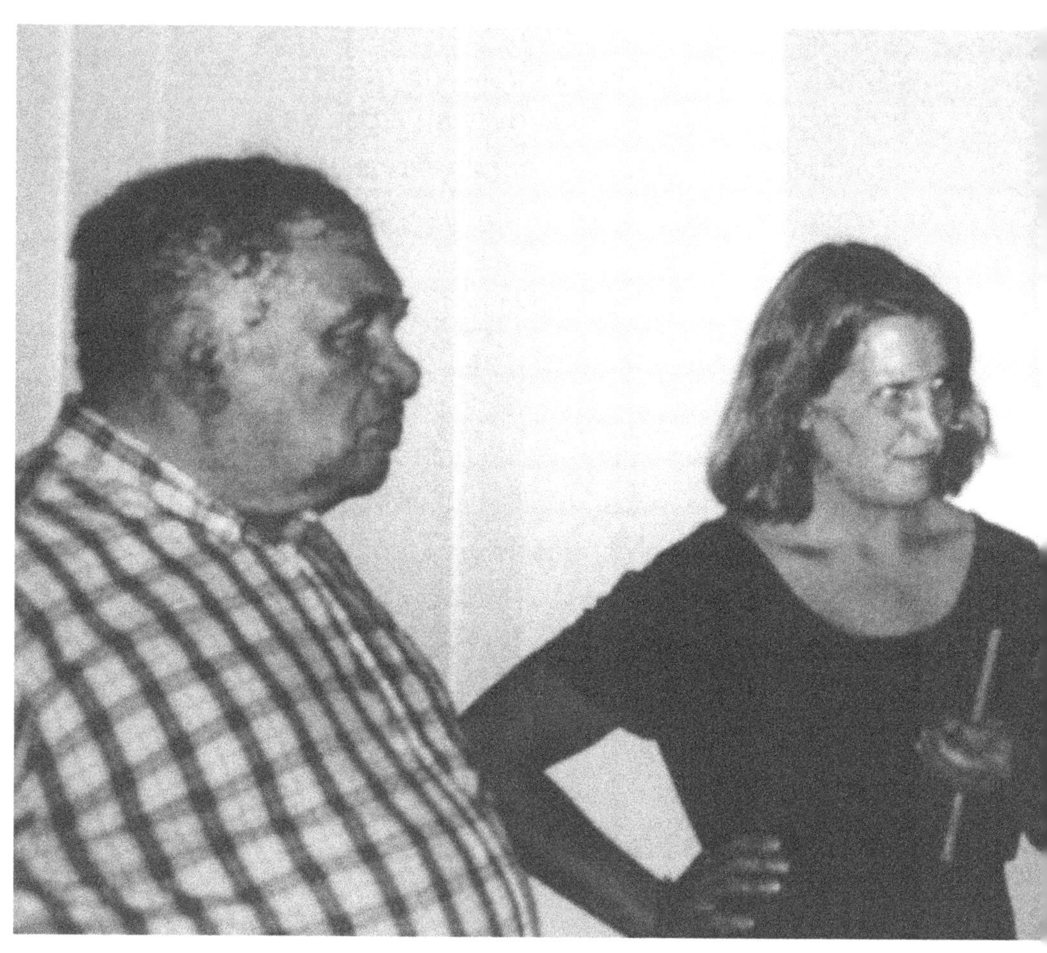

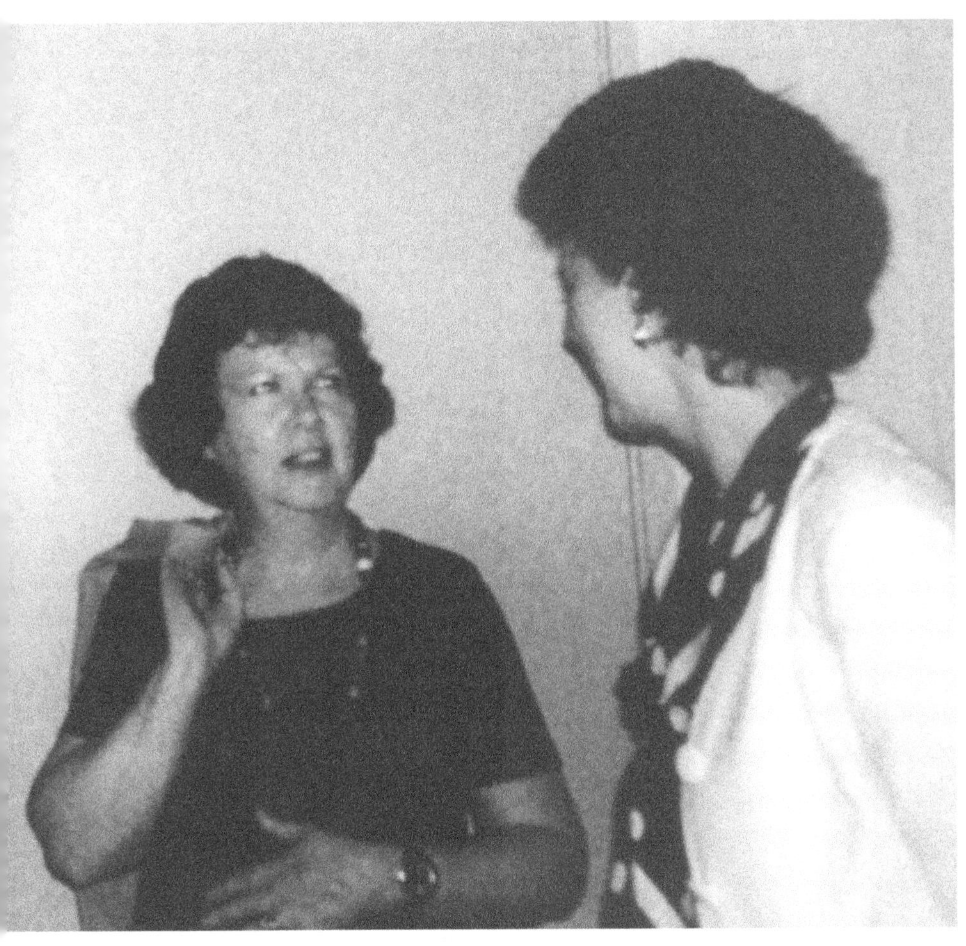

Paolozzi with course administrator Geraldine Prince (right) and staff members of the Scottish Museum of Mankind in Edinburgh

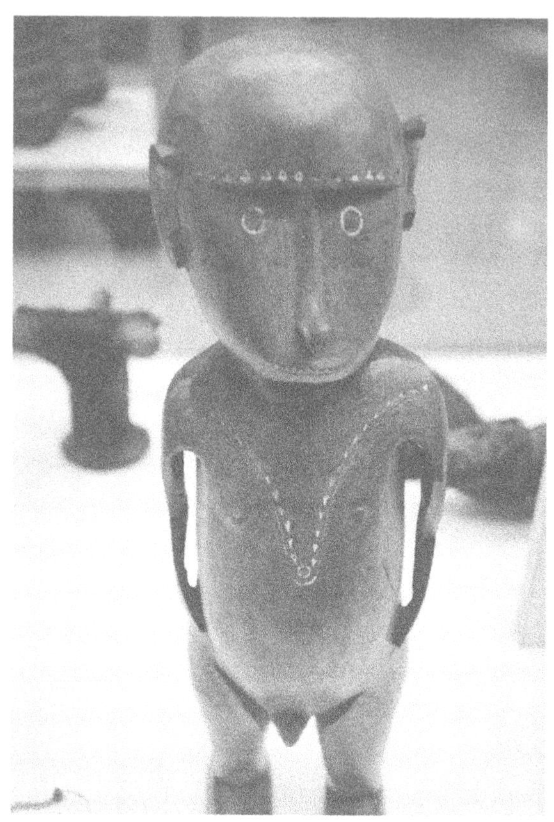

Some examples of primitive art in the museum

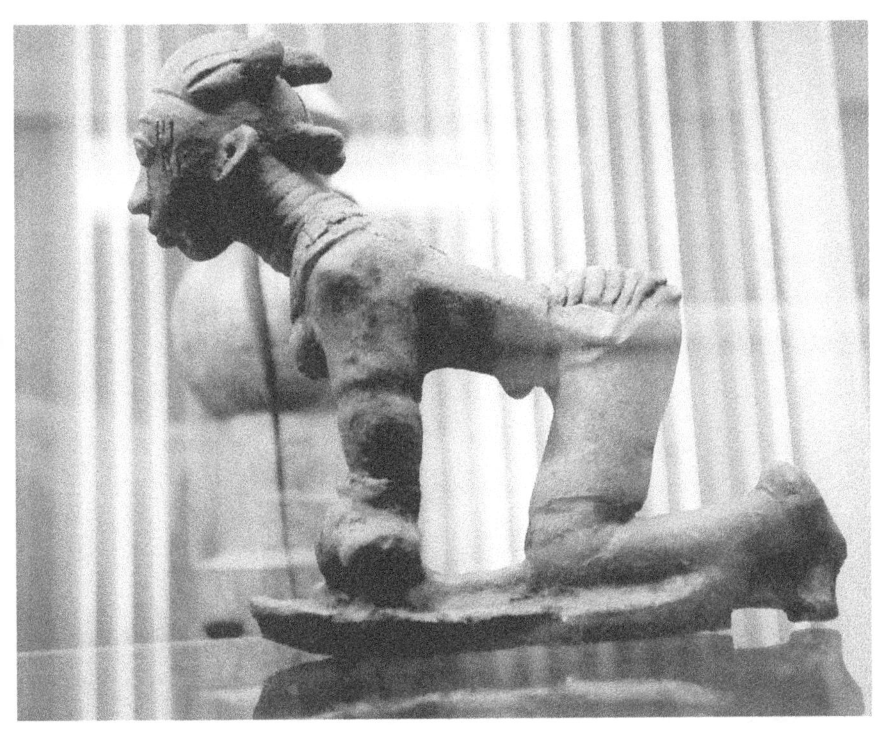

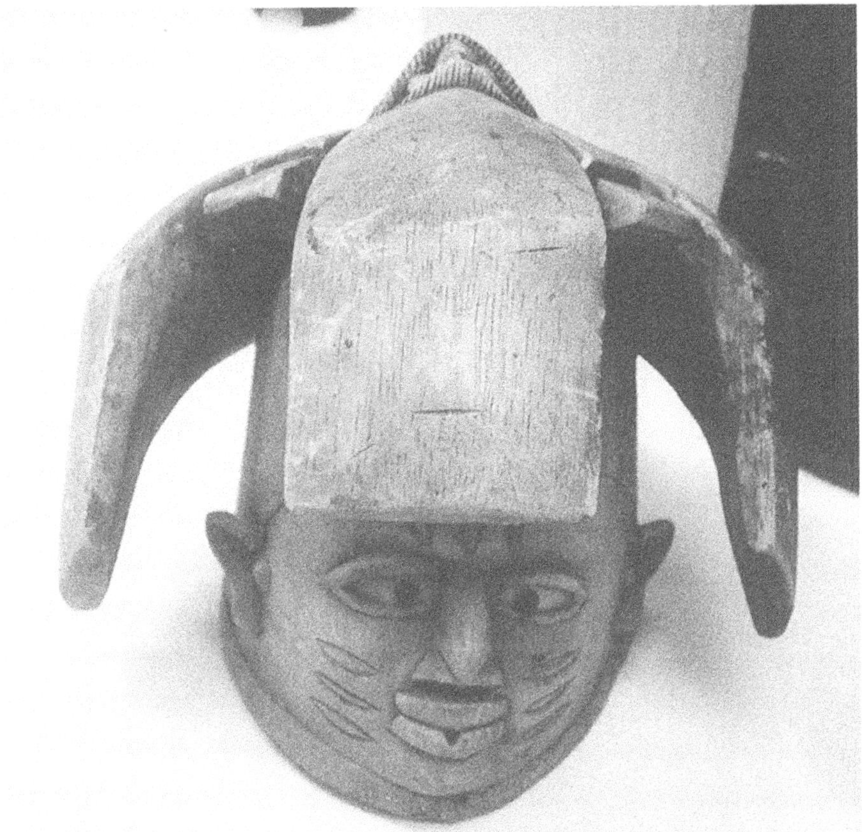

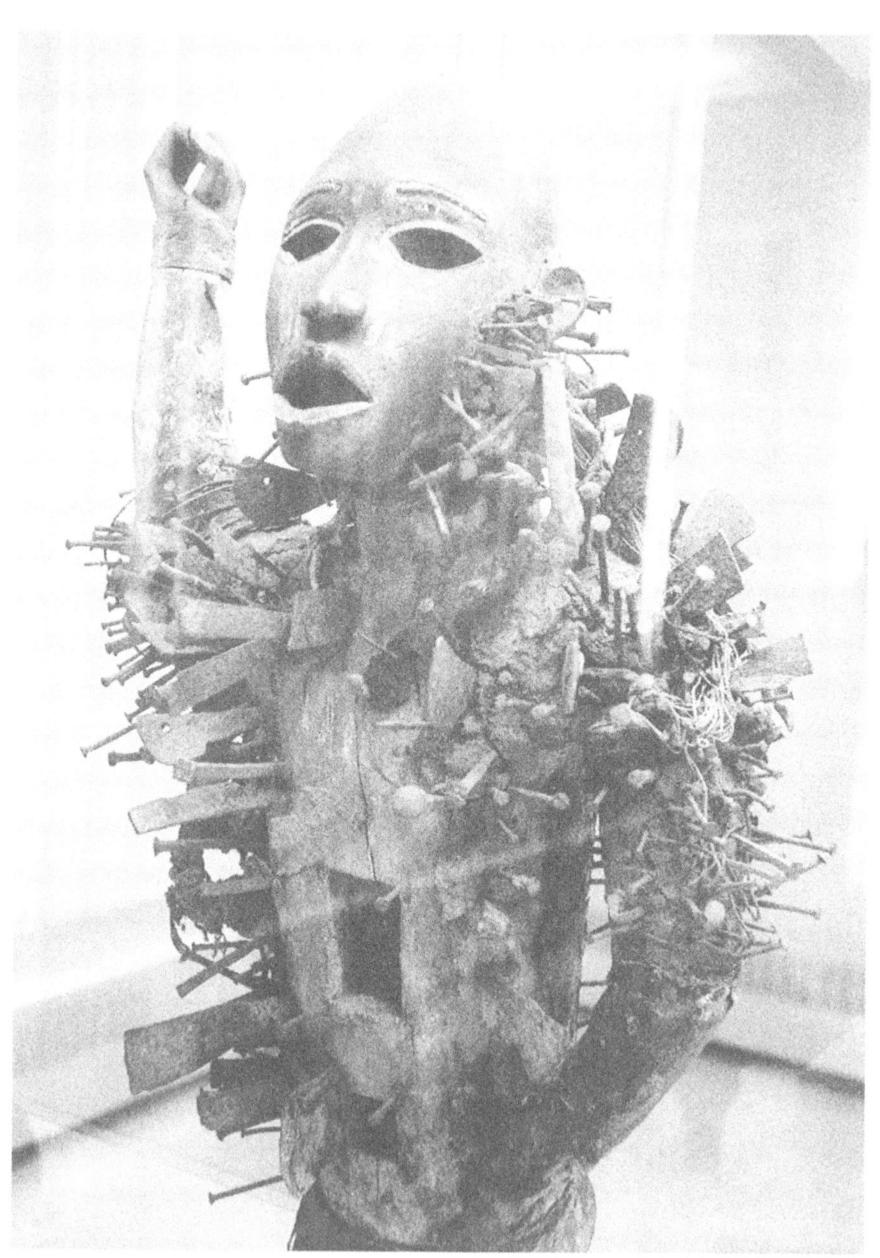

Day Eight

“Rational order in the technological world can be as fascinating as the fetishes of a Congo witch-doctor – scientific phenomena become significant images.”

- Paolozzi

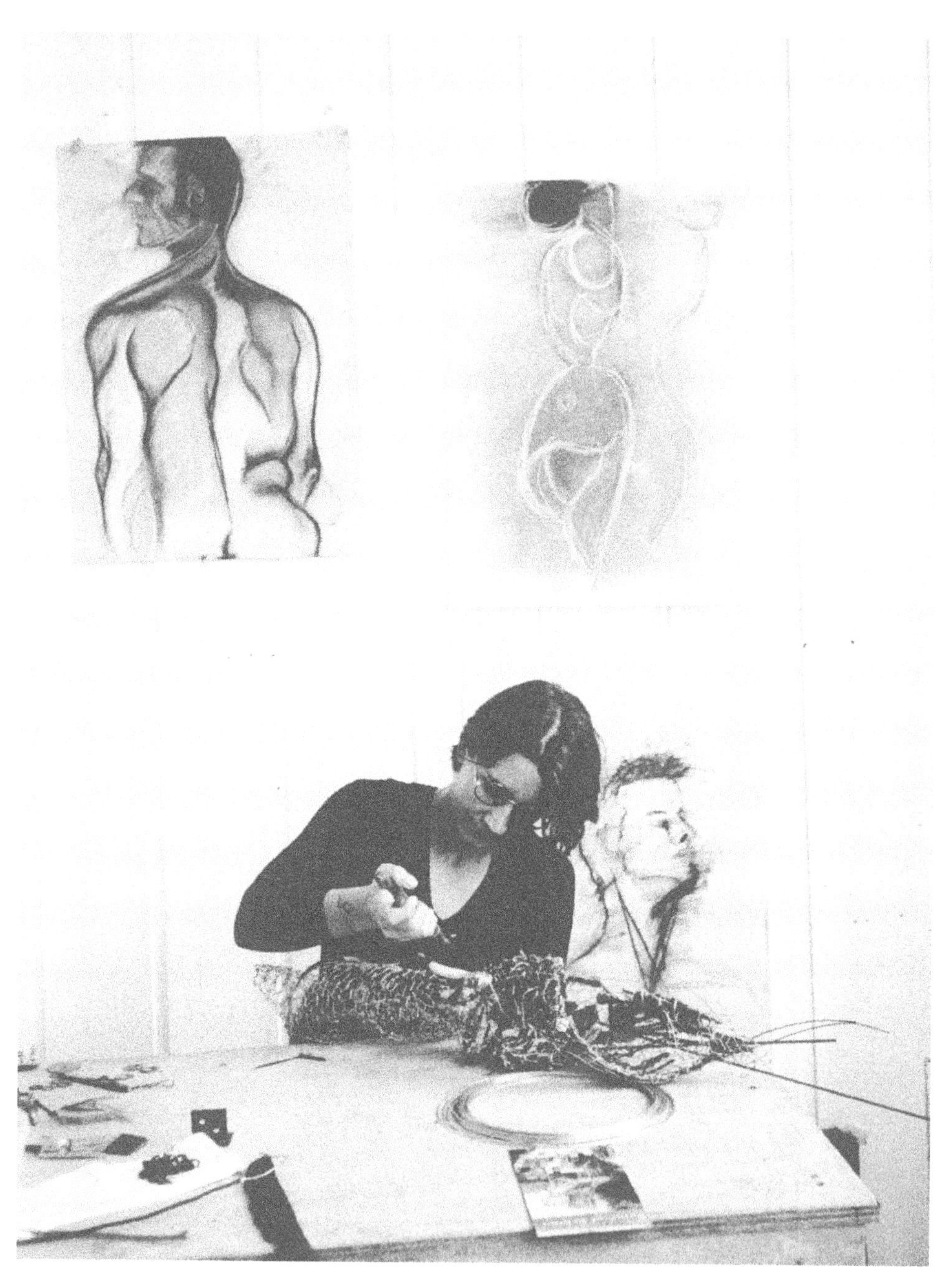

Students were highly prolific and diverse in the work they created.

I return to the library for books on Paolozzi. There are plenty. One art historian refers to him as taking the detritus of a mechanistic world, and the timelessness of a totem, to make something new, and that he brings back strange objects charged with magic.

In one studio discussion he re-asserts this. "I believe in magic," he said. Surely he does not believe in witchcraft? Nobody dares challenge him though. On the previous day, we had visited the National Gallery of Scotland looking at primitive art.

Yet in a strange way I do know what he is talking about. He is referring to the way objects can change in a studio, how in the hands of artists they become infused with a kind of magic and something new is created out of the mundane. Surrealism has been an all-embracing influence on his work. "Anything goes," he says.

Herbert Read's 1964 *Concise History of Modern Sculpture* (Thames & Hudson) gives a clear analysis of Paolozzi's work and his place in the canon of art:

> "Among the hundreds of sculptors who have emerged since 1945, it seems to me that there is only one who might claim to have invented a new style - Eduardo Paolozzi. This is not to discount the originality of sculptors like Cesar, Robert Muller, Fritz Wotruba, Germaine Richier, Theodore Roszak, Berto Lardera, Richard Lippold and many others; but it is possible to make original contributions to an existing movement, which I think all these

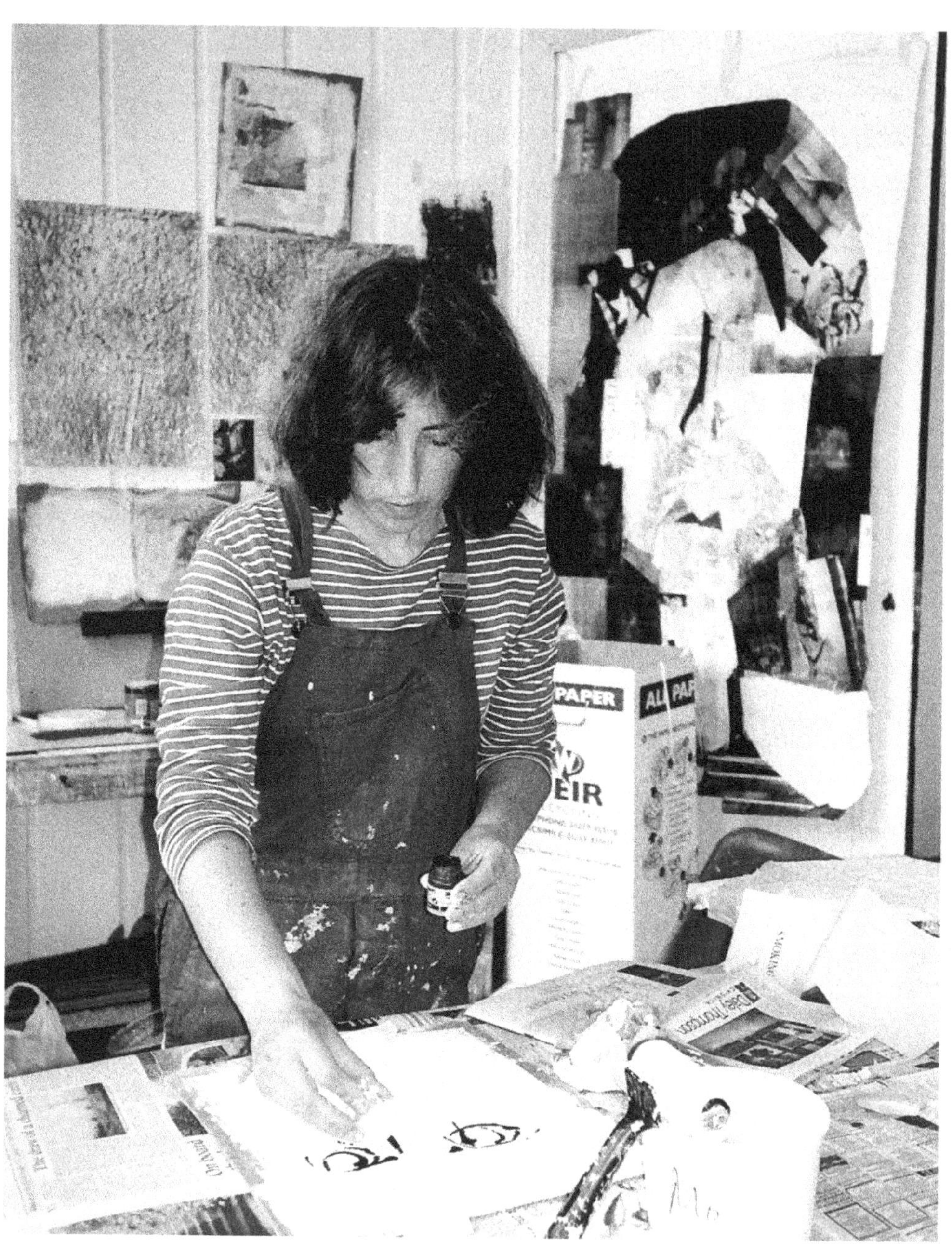
PAPER

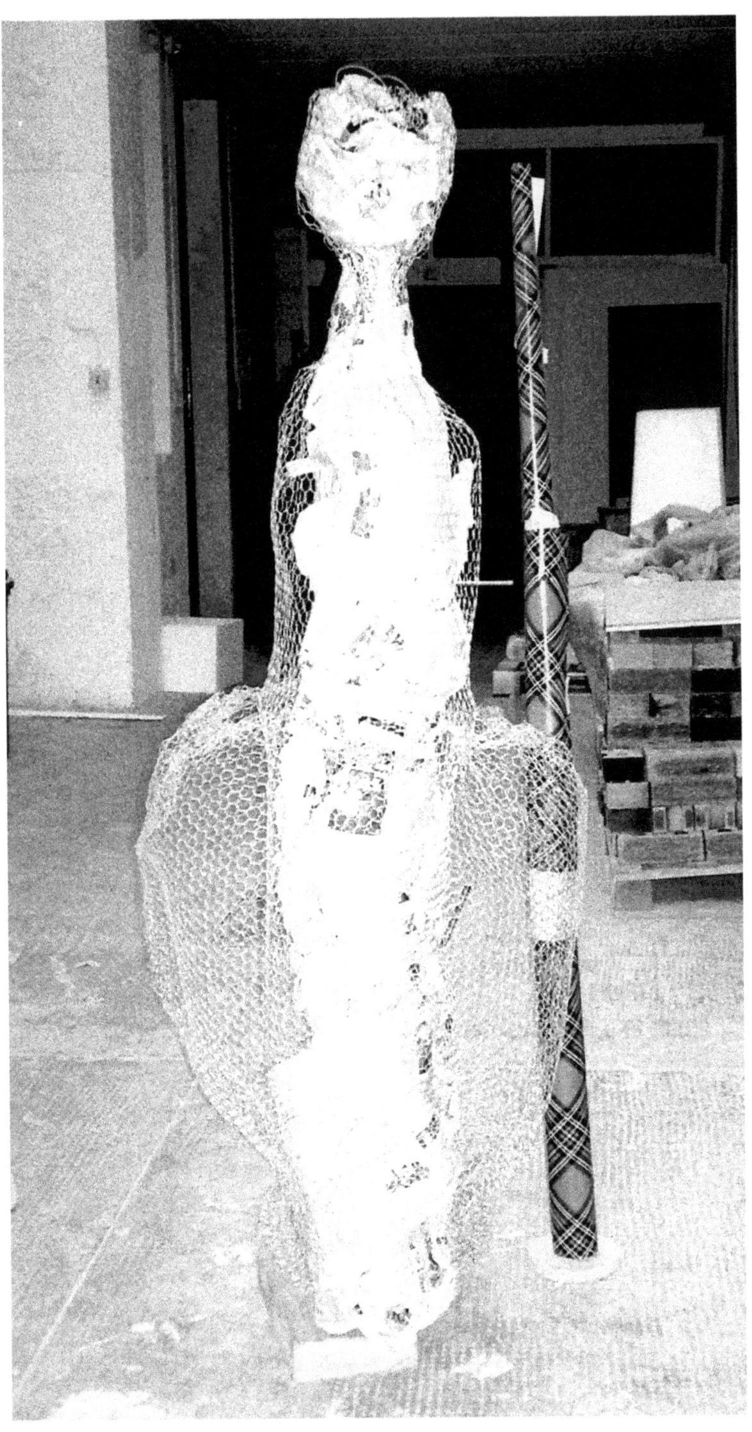

Armature for sculpture - Self Portrait - Ann Shaw

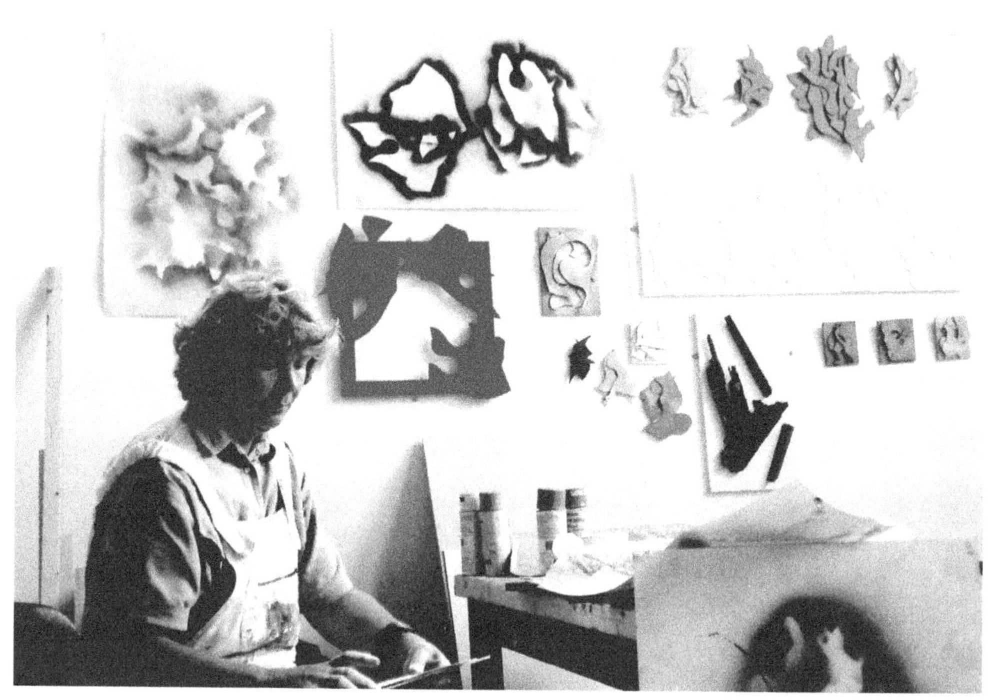

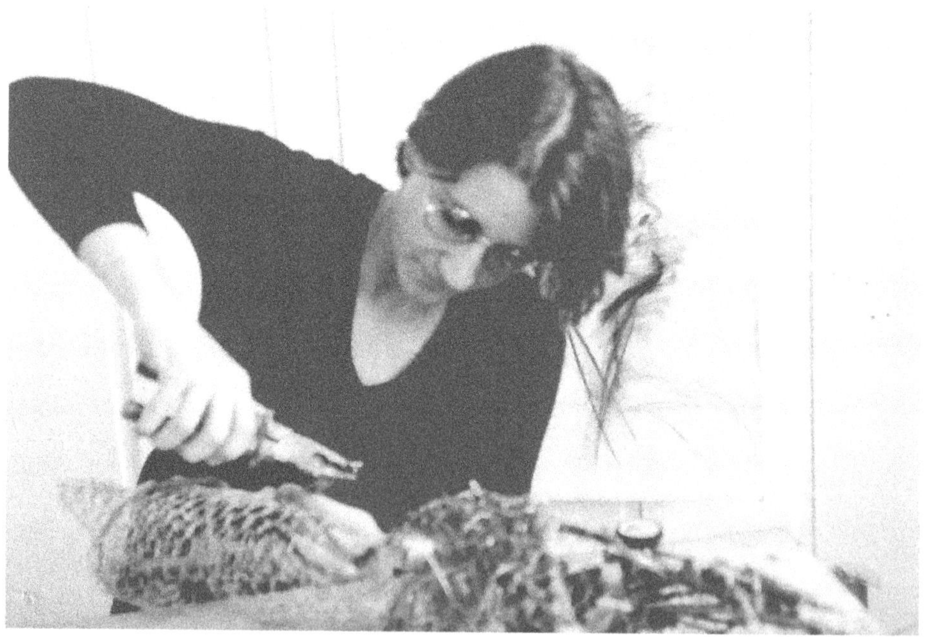

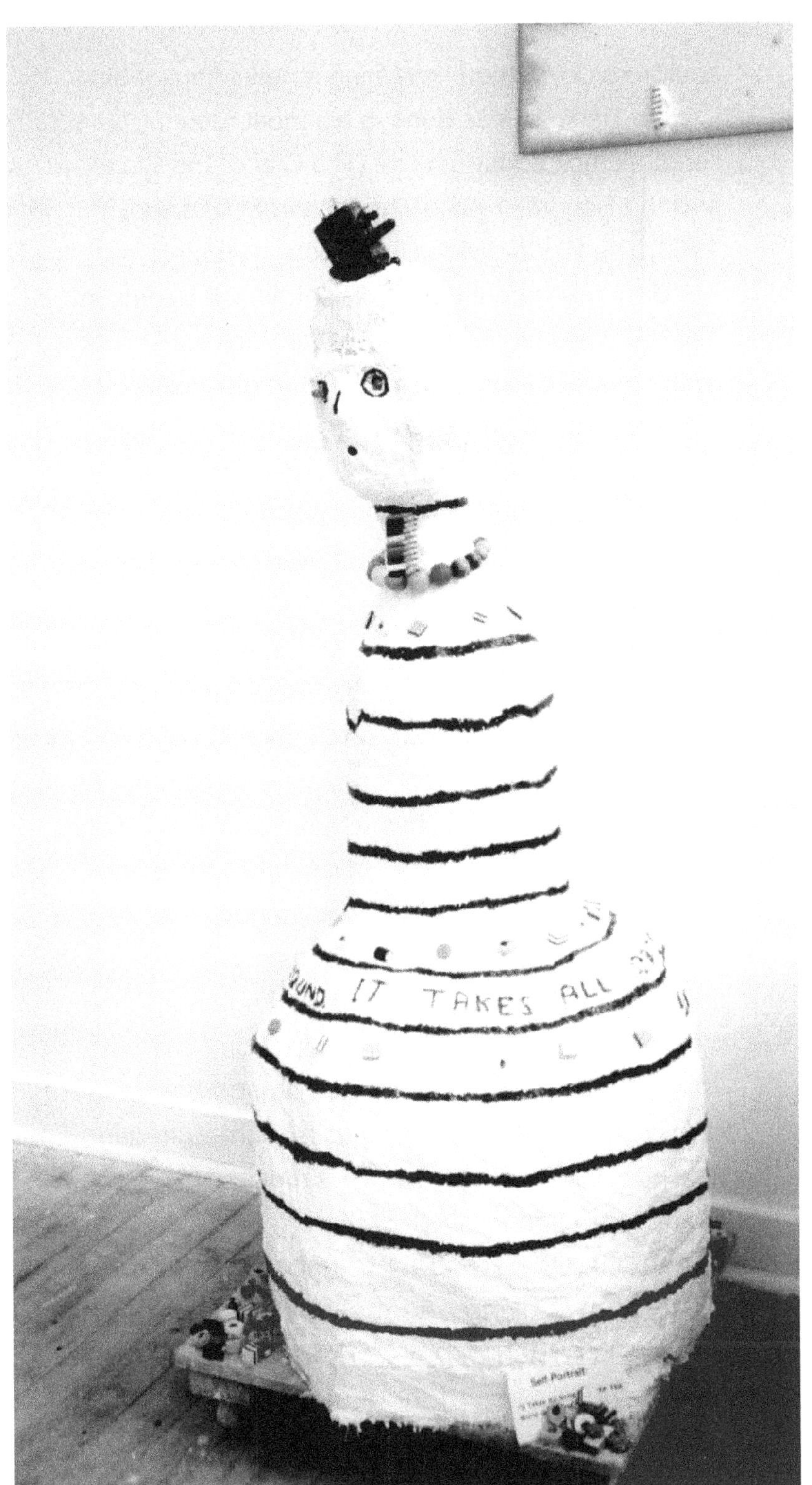

"Self portrait" - Ann Shaw

sculptors do, without inventing a new idiom, which is what Paolozzi has done in his most recent "engineered" constructions (The City of the Circle and the Square, 1963; Wittgenstein at Cassino, 1963; The World divides into Facts, 1963; etc).

"Until this recent development, which begins in 1961, it was still possible to relate Paolozzi's work to the work of Richier or Cesar, and ultimately to Picasso's (Baboon and Young, 1951). But his new images, functionless machine tools or sterile computers, derive not, like his previous work, from the debris of industrialism, but from the rational order of technology.

"I have already quoted his statement that idols representing such an order can be as fascinating as the fetishes of a Congo witch doctor, but a mechanical fetish does not have the same function as a tribal fetish - or rather, it 'functions' in a totally different kind of society, a society whose mental processes aspire to logical consistency.

"By naming some of these constructions 'idols', Paolozzi gives further encouragement to an animistic interpretation of his work; but what is consistent is the realized or incorporate contradiction: as if the mechanical computer had finally achieved a soul, and with that apotheosis ceased to function as a machine."

Meanwhile the emotional temperature in the plaster room is rising. As the week draws to an end there is a rush to get work finished. We arrive to find Camilla's sculpture, a huge plaster self-portrait, broken. She had worked on it until 3 am this morning. She arrives at 11 and is given the bad news. Not surprisingly she bursts into tears.

Martin, one of the duo responsible for the accident, does not bother to apologize. He says "Why not turn this accident to your advantage and create something new?" (He too has become imbued with Paolozzi's influence.)

Camilla is not consoled. She cries more loudly. We shrug and leave her to it. We have our own problems. Some of us work late in the studio. Again I am aware that something is happening in the group. We are all deeply immersed in our own projects, finding ourselves on an inner journey, an adventure of our own making.

Eddie, the janitor, says we can work on after 9 pm. An hour later I am still painting when he returns. He takes the paintbrush out of my hand and shows me the 'correct' way to paint. (I am putting a sealing paint on my life-size plaster self-portrait sculpture.)

"I wonder what Paolozzi would say if he could see you now." Eddie ignores my comment. He is too busy, engrossed in painting. And that perhaps is part of the magic of creating work. One loses oneself in the process.

Earlier we had been to a slide show and discussion where film-maker Murray Grigor interviewed Paolozzi before an invited audience. Paolozzi hates these events. It's full of the great and good of Edinburgh, and Murray Grigor has a tough job interviewing him.

He is a difficult person to interview but having to explain his work before a posh Edinburgh audience wanting an evening of 'culture' is irksome and we find ourselves sympathising with his predicament. Having worked alongside him all week we know that however much there is a need for an artist to talk and promote his own work this is not something Paolozzi enjoys naturally. He would much prefer to be in his studio working or with like-minded artists and writers.

I see a familiar figure in the audience: a colleague of mine, Clare Henry, art critic for *The Glasgow Herald*. We chat about Paolozzi. She says: "He is always amazing us by re-inventing himself." I tell how he had refused to let the media into his Masterclass earlier in the week. She is not surprised. "He has become very anti-media in recent years but I don't understand why."

I think I do, but do not tell her so.

Earlier the principal of Edinburgh Art College, introducing the evening, said: "You can't teach art. All you can do is to provide an environment in which art can be produced." And that is precisely what this Masterclass has been about. Those artists who came expecting an instant kit from Paolozzi, the Grand Old Master of British Sculpture, on 'how to be a successful artist' are disappointed. Art is an adventure, an exploration that you take alone. And in a way that is what Eddie, the janitor, was doing when he picked up my paintbrush.

Day Nine

" I seek to stress all that is wonderful or ambiguous in the most ordinary objects ... I try to subject these objects, which are the basic materials to more than one metamorphosis."

- Paolozzi

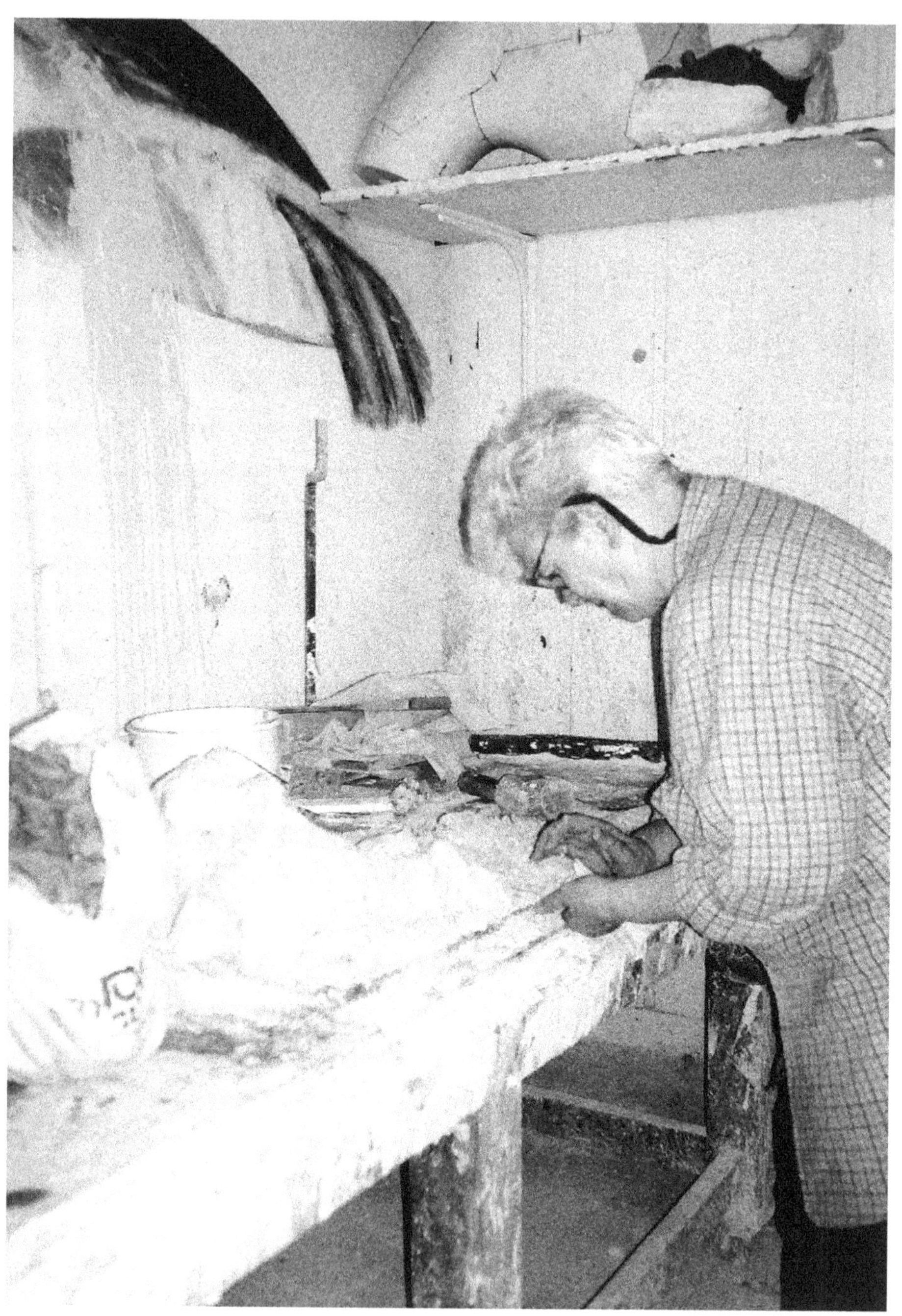

Ten of us cram into the college minibus to take us to Heriot Watt University's Department of computing and engineering on the outskirts of Edinburgh. We are treated like royalty because of Paolozzi's presence. We bask in this reflected glory. Is this what it is like to be famous? This is a million miles away from the hard graft of life in a studio. This is more like it, I think to myself. Then I realise this is what for some of my life I have enjoyed as a journalist, for the weight of a newspaper behind one gives you automatic kudos and doors open seamlessly once the magic words *The Glasgow Herald* are uttered.

And here I am about to give all that up to try and fulfil a lifelong ambition to be an artist, to spend the rest of my life in a studio, probably alone, and with little prospect of reward either financial or fame, and I wonder if I am making the right decision. Do I have the commitment to become an artist?

The university wants to show Paolozzi how artists and sculptors in the future can work with computing and engineering departments to create totally new kinds of sculpture, work which we have never so far imagined. We have been promised we will be able to go into 'virtual reality'.

Paolozzi is not sure what this means. He is the first to don the helmet and leave the physical world for the virtual one. We watch his reactions. There are none. He is non-committal, though he shows a bit more interest later, when he learns that technically it would be possible to have sex with Raquel Welch in 'virtual reality'.

I am wildly enthusiastic about virtual reality, and its possibilities, and I can't wait to get the helmet on to see exactly what our future, or one aspect of our future will be like. In the briefing we get before entering the laboratory, university staff explain that in this new world one is limited only by one's imagination and no longer by the envelope of the materials one uses. We are allocated cyber guides to take us around. They keep uttering phrases such as "You will fly, not walk, around the room."

I am first in the queue. Meanwhile the other students remain lukewarm in their interest in technology, still convinced that this is 'not proper art'. Once I get the helmet on it is every bit as mind-boggling as I had expected. In this virtual space I am able to whizz around from room to room totally airborne. After a few minutes I hear the voice of Martin, the doctor, urging me to hand over the helmet for the rest of the students. Then came Paolozzi's voice quietly: "Leave her alone."

A minute passed, or maybe a few, because time had little meaning in this new world unfolding before my eyes, and again Martin's voice could be heard urging me to hand over the helmet, and again Paolozzi intervened. "Leave her alone. She's playing."

And that is exactly what I was doing. I was playing in virtual reality. He understood, in a way that only artists do, the importance of play - especially in the creative process.

We are introduced to a Ph.D. student doing a thesis on the ethics of virtual reality and its potential to change human behaviour. The visit concludes with Paolozzi inviting Patricia Erskine from the Department of Mechanical and Chemical Engineering to visit us tomorrow.

Despite his reputation for being awkward and anti-social he is carefully attuned to the need and importance of networking and recognises the importance of establishing links between what seem at first glance to be such very different areas of expertise.

In the evening we are invited to an informal lecture where he shows us slides of his work in the metal workshop. Nick, his assistant, runs the slide show. One slide is of a visiting professor in Berlin dressed in drag. It is an extraordinary image of a young man with a smirk on his face, naked except for what seems some strange-feathered headgear straight from some African tribal art, black fishnet tights, and a leather suspender belt revealing orange pubic hair. We stare at the image in silence, not knowing what to say. A week ago we would have burst out laughing.

Finally one student says: "Does he normally dress like this?" "No," replied Paolozzi. We wonder why we have been shown this image. Is it to shake up our middle-class bourgeois view of life that treats art as a comfortable commodity, a decoration for our homes or, worse, a status symbol?

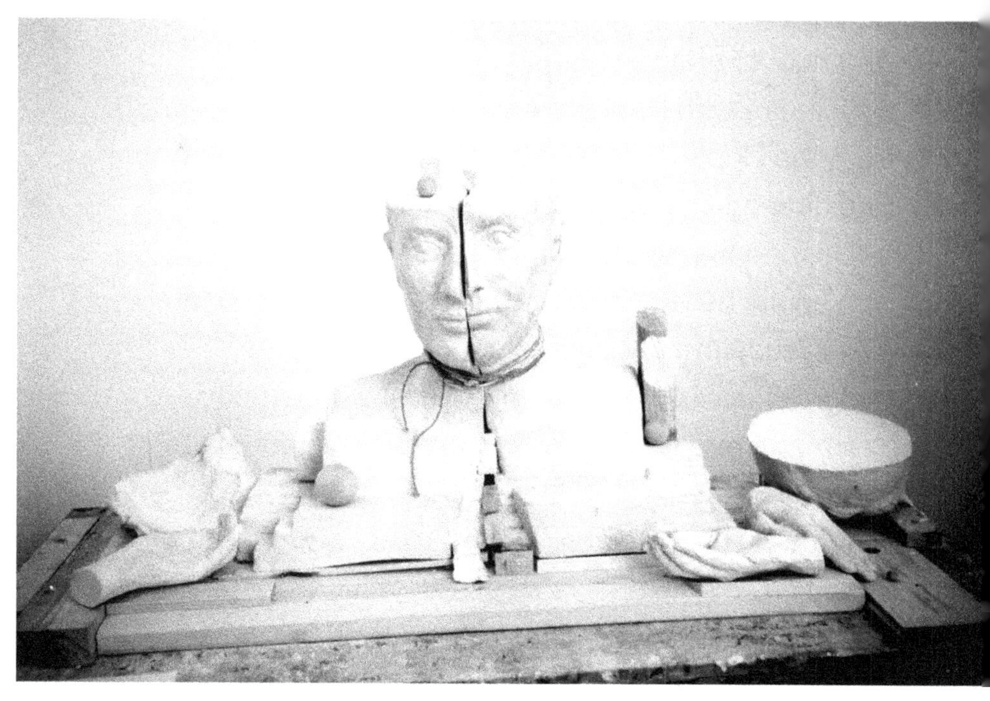

Day Ten

" There are no rules."

- *Paolozzi*

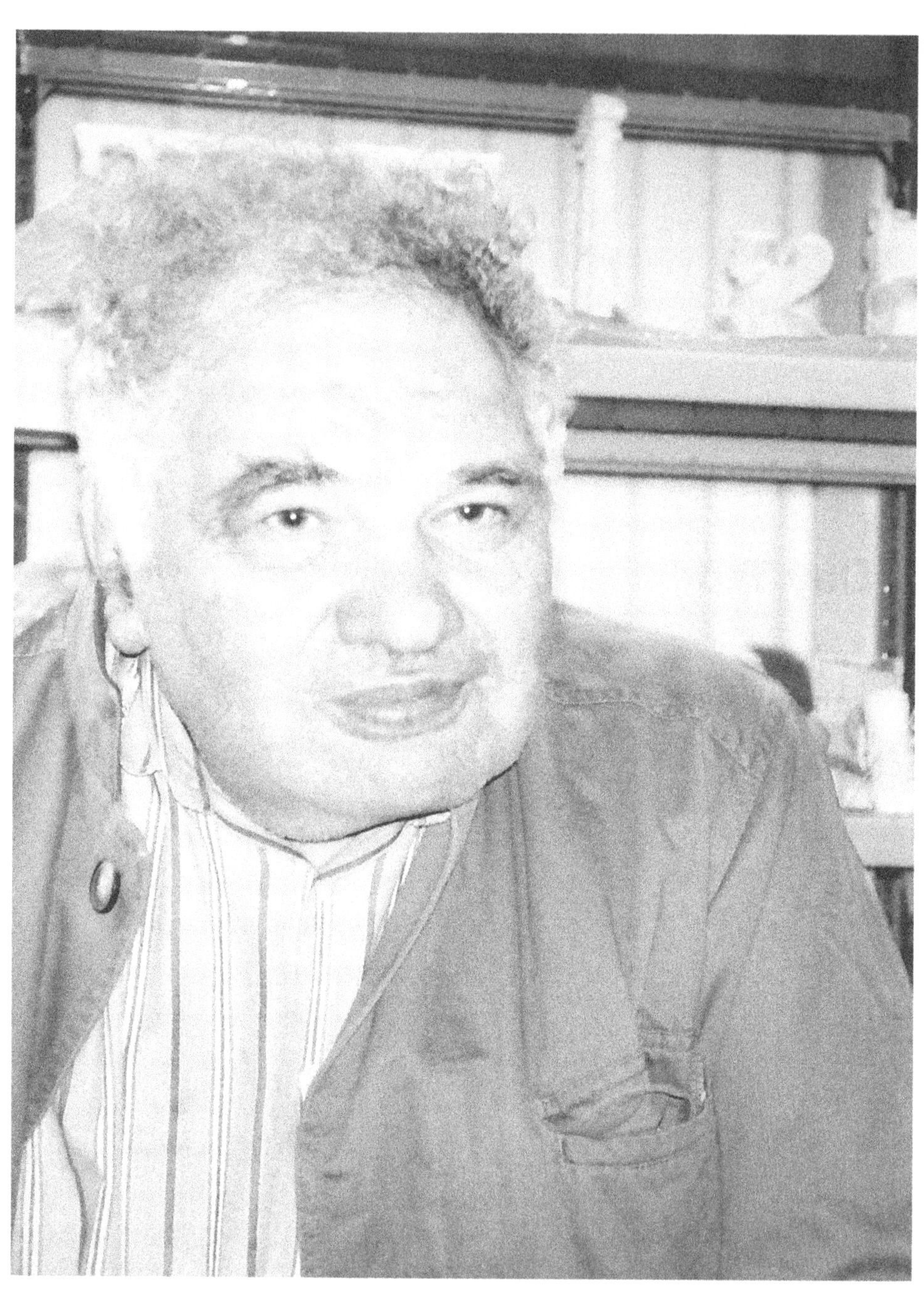

Paolozzi in his Leith workshop

Final day. We catch a glimpse of Paolozzi's ferocious temper, and experience his generosity. And I am the cause of the vitriolic outburst, which leaves the studio stunned. We are taken to visit an industrial unit in Leith, which is the temporary home for Paolozzi's work while refurbishment to the newly acquired Dean Centre, an extension to the Scottish National Gallery of Art, is completed.

It will be dedicated to Paolozzi, a final recognition and tribute in his own home town, for Edinburgh society never fully embraced this Italian-Scot working-class sculptor, even though he has enjoyed an international reputation for many years. Today he is recognised within the canon of art as a major 20th century sculptor, so they can no longer ignore this son of an Italian immigrant worker living in Leith.

From the outside the unit looks just like all the others on this modern industrial estate. But once inside we step into Paolozzi's studio with shelves packed to the ceiling lined with casts of his work.

It's an extraordinary sight. I take photographs, something I have been doing all week. Now on the final day I thought it would be good to have one of Paolozzi, also I feel confident enough now to think he would approve.

He is talking to some students and as he turns I ask him to look at the camera.

It's as if I have ignited a stick of dynamite. He verbally attacks me, the details of it all I can only vaguely remember because I am too shocked. It

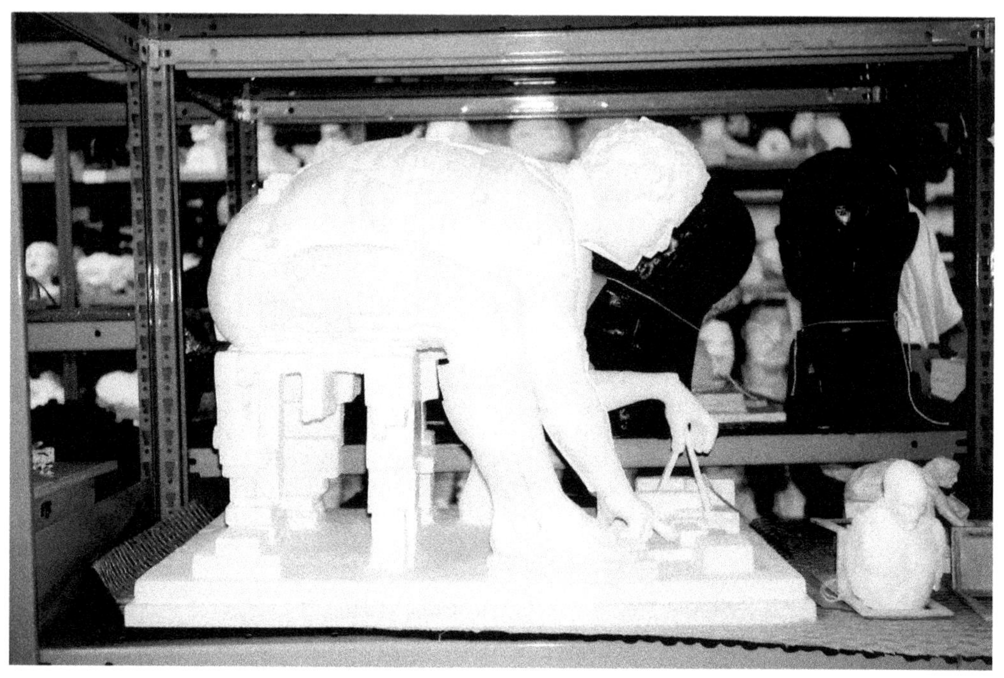

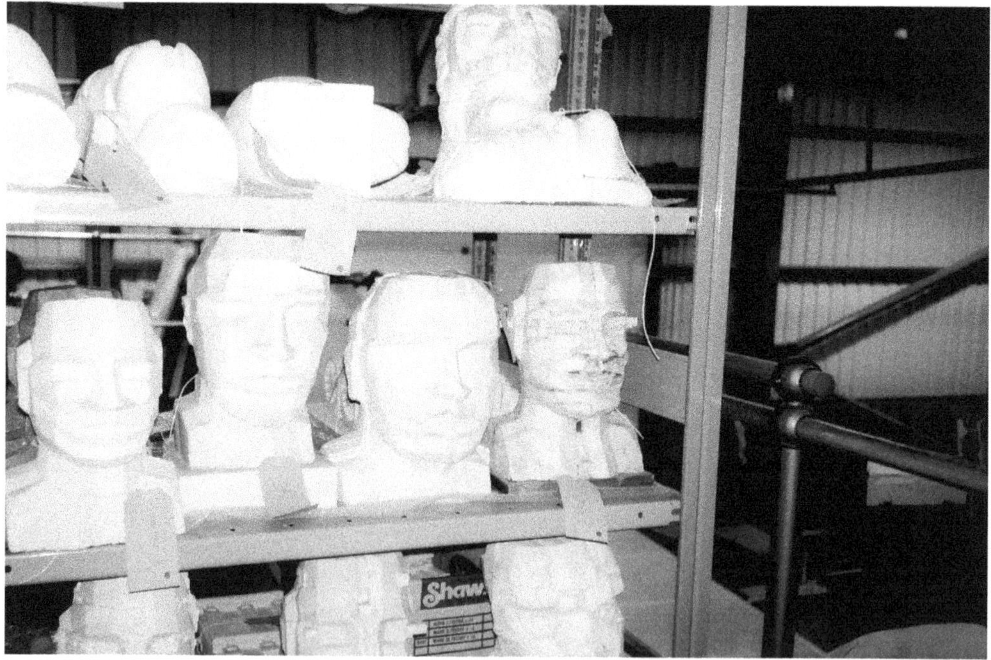

 Inside Paolozzi's Leith workshop/storage unit.

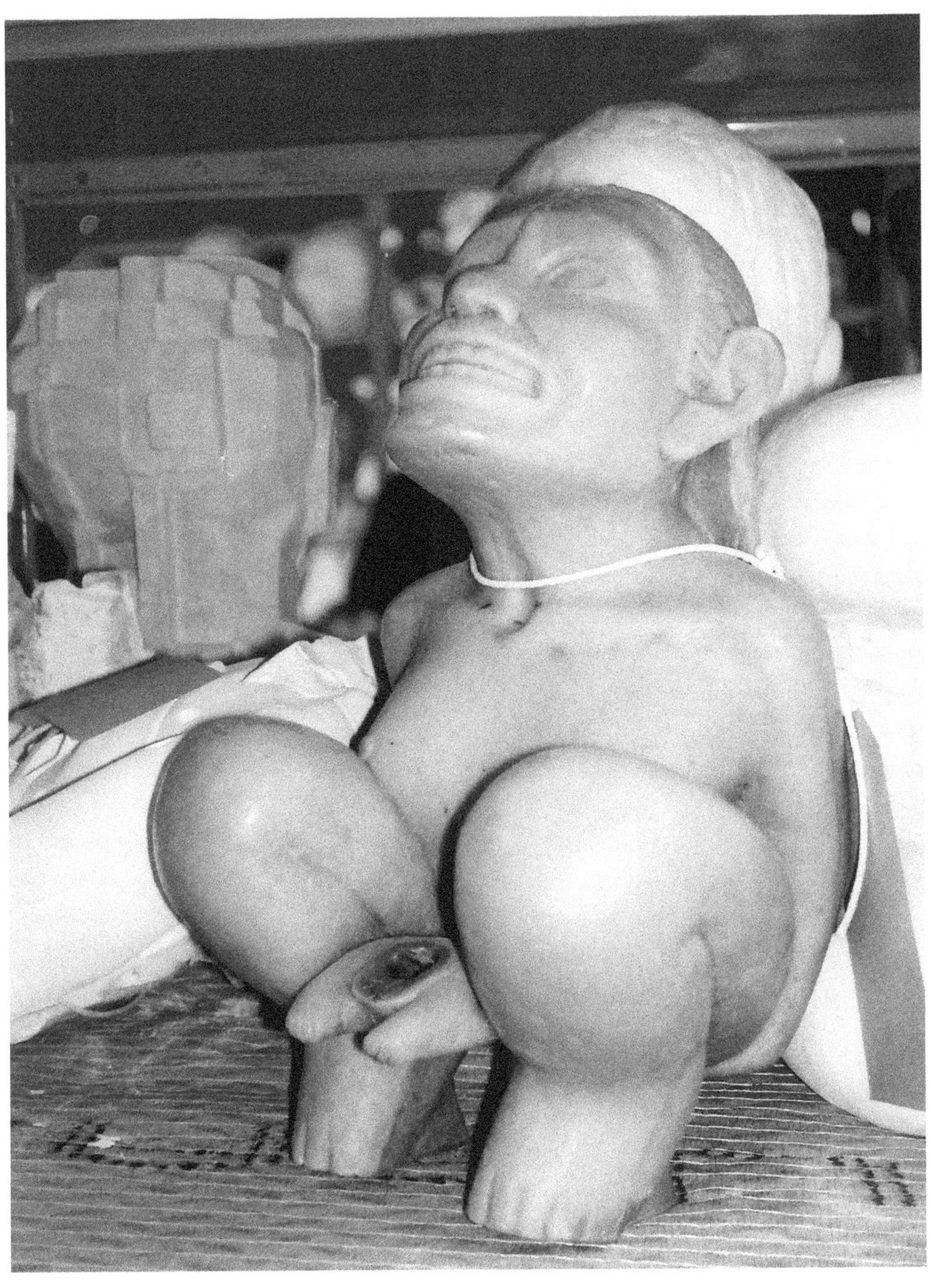

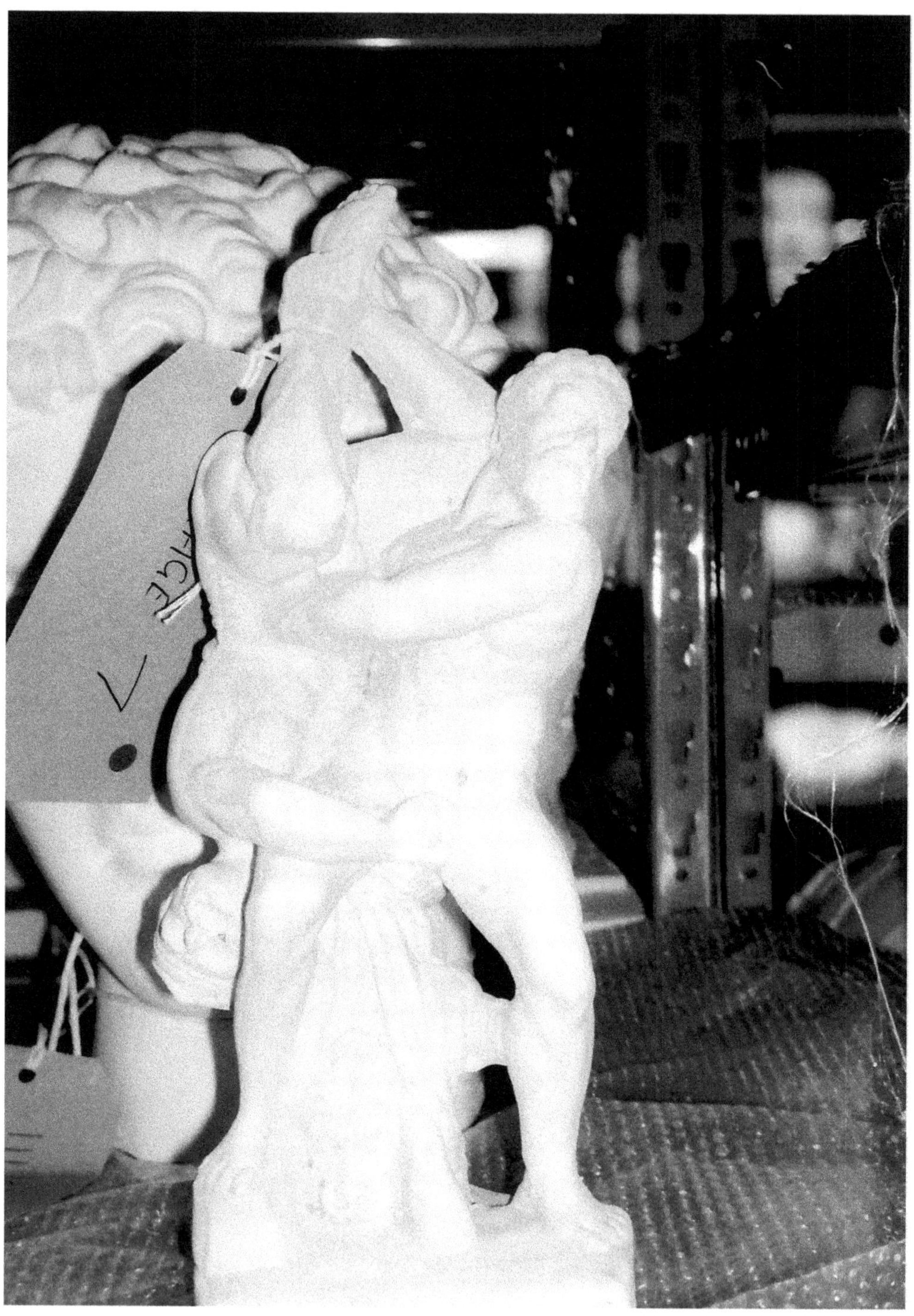

centres on the fact that I ask too many questions. (Well, I am a journalist, for God's sake!) It is as if I had irritated him all week and he could no longer contain his real emotions.

For the first time we see the other side of Paolozzi, the figure that has intimidated some sections of the art establishment for years. There is a stunned silence. Nobody speaks. Then Geraldine steps forward and moves the group on. Should I apologise? I had assumed he would have no objection to one photo because all week I had been photographing everybody else in the studio. Only now I become stubborn. I will not say sorry. I walk away.

This unfortunate incident mars the end of the Masterclass though some of the old camaraderie returns later that evening when we all go out together for a meal in an Edinburgh restaurant. After all we have grown into a close-knit group.

But Paolozzi sits alone in silence. I make certain I have a table as far away from him as possible. Every so often I catch him looking in my direction. No words are spoken. I regret the incident, which spoiled an otherwise extraordinary week.

Later Geraldine announces there will not be a special prize for the best in class. Instead everyone will receive a signed plaster head by Paolozzi. She adds: "If anyone thinks they have not had value for money on this course then they can sell it."

My ten days working with Paolozzi taught me that art is about freedom. In his own words: "follow your obsessions."

At the end of the course Paolozzi gave us each a signed plaster head..

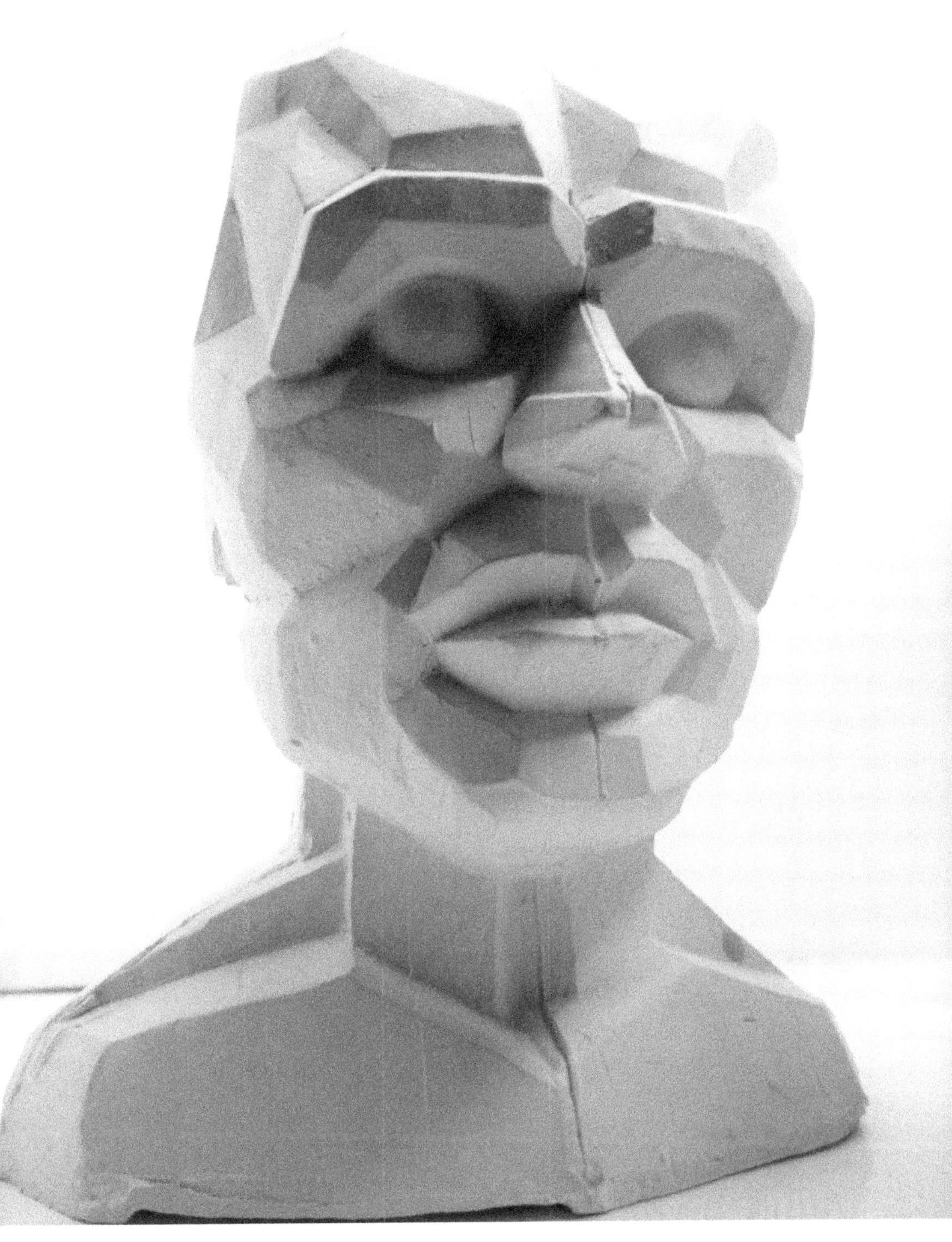

www.ingramcontent.com/pod-product-compliance
Ingram Content Group UK Ltd.
Pitfield, Milton Keynes, MK11 3LW, UK
UKHW020427250726
13967UKWH00007B/2836